P9-CQD-366

DON'T BE A STRANGER

Don't Be a STRANGER

Create Your Own Luck
in Business through
Strategic Relationship Building

LAWRENCE R. PERKINS

LIONCREST
PUBLISHING

COPYRIGHT © 2020 LAWRENCE R. PERKINS
All rights reserved.

DON'T BE A STRANGER
Create Your Own Luck in Business through
Strategic Relationship Building

ISBN 978-1-5445-0965-5 *Hardcover*
     978-1-5445-0964-8 *Paperback*
     978-1-5445-0963-1 *Ebook*
     978-1-5445-0966-2 *Audiobook*

CONTENTS

INTRODUCTION

The other day, my friend Todd told me that his email had gotten hacked. "Best thing that's happened to me in years," he said.

Todd is a private investor. He works for a company that invests billions of dollars in various projects. The entire business is relationship-based. Todd and I have been friends for years, and he's built a huge network of relationships. He has more than three thousand contacts in his address book.

When the email was hacked, the hackers sent out an email to everyone on Todd's contact list. Three thousand copies of the email asked people to wire money to China in the most rudimentary language possible. Of course, no one in his entire list thought he'd sent it, so no one clicked. What's amazing was how many people started writing back anyway.

"Todd! It's been so long since I've heard from you. Looks

like you were hacked, but we should absolutely catch up sometime. How are you doing?" People he'd met in college twenty-five years ago were reaching out to do lunch. Suddenly Todd had a calendar full of activities with highly accomplished people who already thought of him fondly. Thirty of them had business opportunities perfect for his firm.

Todd filled up his pipeline with hundreds of millions of dollars of opportunities as a direct result of that day. When he told me the story, he laughed and said he wished his email would get hacked once a year.

THAT MISERABLE COCKTAIL PARTY

When I was twenty-nine years old, I showed up at a terrible networking event at a cheesy restaurant. I had just started my business six days before, and I figured this was the kind of thing business owners go to. I listened to one sales pitch after another, had bad drinks and no food, and walked around trying to talk to someone interesting—with little success.

Sometime during that interminable cocktail party, I stuck out my hand and introduced myself to Gabriel. He was an independent lawyer working for an eponymous firm doing mergers and acquisitions. I got his card and followed up with an email the next day (mostly because I didn't have my own cards yet). We had breakfast shortly thereafter and hit it off.

Eventually he invited me to a dinner he hosted to connect people in his circle, and four months later he called me with a client who could use my services.

From that small job I met Robert. Robert hired me for consulting work, and when I did a good job, he introduced me to Lindsay. Then Lindsay introduced me to Will. All four of these guys did business with me over the next few years. They helped me. I helped them, both doing what I do for a living and helping them outside of my profession. For example, I introduced several of their friends to their current employers.

Will eventually introduced me to the folks that bought my first company. Among the four of them, they've brought me tens of millions of dollars of business. We've had countless lunches and dinners and business deals, and we've become real friends along the way. One of them hosted my bachelor party.

One business card at a miserable networking event transformed my life.

STUCK IN THE MAZE

It's terrible being stuck on the corporate ladder. I've been there. You're walking past the Hudson bookstore in the airport, on your way to someplace you really don't want to go.

It's Monday night, and you're tired. You pick up a book, frustrated with your life. You don't want to go to Wichita again. You want to find a way out.

Or maybe you're at the office. You're great at your job, and you're working your butt off. You have a long list of responsibilities, and the client likes you. You're advancing up the corporate ladder. Somehow it feels like it's taking too long. You're slaving away while a business partner comes in to the client site once a month for two hours in the office, some golf, and a steak dinner. How do you get to be *that* guy?

Put a different way, how do you get to be Todd, whose hacked email sends him business? How do you build a life with people who actively help you, like Gabriel and Robert and Lindsay and Will have helped me? I'll give you a hint: it's not by working harder. (At least not in the traditional sense.)

I tried working harder, and it didn't get me far. At twenty-one years old, I set the record for the total number of hours ever worked by a management consultant in our region at our firm. I got in at seven o'clock every morning and usually left at 11:30 pm. Often six or seven days a week. I was exhausted. Meanwhile, my boss was getting in at 9:30 or 10:00, sitting in his office, talking on the phone and laughing for a couple of hours, and then going out for long lunches. He'd come back and give us our assignments for the day and then play golf or go to dinner. His life looked shockingly better than mine. How did he do it while I was working myself to the bone?

I eventually figured out his secret: my boss built his life around the kind of network Todd has, the kind of network I have now. People liked my boss, trusted him, and called him up to give him business. He was also, by the way, an expert at what he did, but his relationships made it possible. Relationships made the phone ring.

I spent the next several years figuring out how to build those same kinds of relationships, that same "book of business" I'd seen so many others leverage to huge success. In this book, I'll teach you how to do exactly that.

It's easier than you think.

DON'T BE A STRANGER

Why don't you follow up with the people you click with?

You have lunch with a friend, someone you like, or just a nice long conversation with someone on the airplane. You say something like, "I had a really great time talking; let's do lunch again." Or you say, "Don't be a stranger." Yet weeks and months and years go by and everyone does, in fact, act like they're strangers.

This book is about ending that cycle. Why not follow up intentionally? Why not do what you said you were going to do? Why not live with integrity? You like the people already—so following up shouldn't be hard.

You just have to do it.

RELATIONSHIPS ARE FOR INTROVERTS, TOO

I like people. I'm gregarious, and I like spending time with friends. I'm also, however, a bit of an introvert, both in practice and according to various personality assessments. How can both be true?

Before every event we go to, my wife and I joke that we don't want to go. Left to my own devices, I'd love to stay home and watch Netflix much of the time. Every time my wife and I go to an event, however, we talk afterward about how happy we are that we went. We talk about the people we've met and enjoyed.

Every time we go, we build another piece of a connection that benefits our lives. So we make ourselves go, and we're glad we do. We've built relationships over the years so that every time we go out, we're spending time with friends.

No one likes going into a room and shaking hands with complete strangers. That's not what this system is about. Instead,

I've learned to build relationships so that when I do go, I go to spend time with friends. It feels good, despite the energy it takes to get there.

I've found that people make my life richer. I learned to reach out and build relationships, first informally and then on purpose with the system I'll teach you. I learned to value and appreciate people, not just for the things they could bring into my life, but for their own sake, too. People make my life better.

Maybe you're an introvert, too, and perhaps even more of an introvert than I am. You can still learn to build connections that enrich your life. It may not feel as natural as you'd like in the beginning, but even if you're barely off first base, you'll be able to pick up new skills faster than you imagine. You'll be able to build a life rich in people.

If you're already good at building relationships, or you're an extrovert, that's fine, too! What I'll show you in this book will help you leverage the skills you already have to expand your network. This system is for everyone.

Best of all, it's not actually hard. Once you have the skills, connecting with people becomes an enjoyable, easy part of your day that pays huge dividends—if you keep doing it.

STRATEGIC SERENDIPITY

In case having more enjoyable people in your life wasn't enough on its own, there's also a strong business case for not being a stranger.

Many—if not most—businesses are what I call "event driven." An event happens, and the person needs a particular kind of help. Take lawyers, for example: most people don't need a lawyer every day. When an event suddenly causes someone to seek out a lawyer, they're going to call the lawyer they've heard of, the one they liked.

We'd all rather do business with people we like and trust. Skills matter, too—everyone wants to hire someone who does a great job for them. Doctors, lawyers, financial advisors, consultants, real estate agents, accountants—and everyone else—have to do great work. Your health, your business, or your future house is on the line. Even if you go to your local sandwich shop and chat with the owner while they make a sandwich, you're trusting them to brighten what could be a mundane part of your day with the excellence of their sandwich-making craft.

That's why relationships matter. If I look for a doctor on my health insurance website, I have no context for who they are or what they're like. Reading their bio or knowing where they went to college and med school tells me nothing about their aptitude, people skills, or whether I can trust them to do a good job as my doctor. If my friend refers me, on the other hand, there's already trust. I know the person she's referring me to is part of a community, and they will care about their reputation in that community. The doctor is already known to do a good job.

By reaching out and building relationships on purpose, through touchpoints, we become the people that other people like and trust. We become top of mind when they need a consultant, lawyer, or a real estate agent. We become the people they'll call first, with the network of people who can vouch for us.

For some reason, in the internet era, people seem to think relationships don't matter anymore. I'd argue they matter more than they ever have. In the era of Instagram, Facebook, and LinkedIn, everyone puts up the highlight reel of his life. It's easy to look like an all-star online. A great website, however, tells you nothing at all about what kind of business you're dealing with. Your friend or your business contact will give you the real story.

Learning to build relationships feels good, and it grows business naturally. When you're the person that everyone remembers, you close more deals. The event in her life happens, and she picks up the phone. You strategically place yourself in the right place to benefit from the business.

Even better, building relationships improves your ability

to do your job. Real estate agents who are highly connected know more about what's going on in their market. They get better prices for the houses they sell and are able to connect their buyers to more houses faster. Being better at their jobs in turn brings in even more business. If their competitors aren't doing the same, they develop a clear strategic advantage.

In this book, I'll teach you how to make luck, or serendipity, work in your favor. There are many lawyers—or accountants, or sandwich makers—in the world. Whatever you do, you will have competition. The key here is that you don't have to be the best in the world to get those calls. You just have to strategically be in the right place at the right time, on purpose.

CONNECTIONS BUILT MY BUSINESS

Discovering how to build relationships on purpose has been the most important thing I have ever done. Connections have built my career and opened up my life, and I want to share the knowledge of how to do it with everyone I can.

I wasn't born a connector. I discovered the system I'll teach you when I quit my job in 2006, when I had decided at twenty-nine years old to start a high-end consulting business.

I knew that everyone more senior than I already had a large

book of business. They could leverage their relationships, pick up the phone, and get business much more easily than I could. Without similar relationships to call on, I was certain I would starve.

Fortunately, nothing motivates like necessity. When my first project was about to end, I saw the credit card bill staring down at me. A mania took over me—how could I get the phone to ring? I tried everything: cold calls, web ads, magazine ads, breakfasts, webinars, conferences, drinks, pens, calendars, toaster ovens. I spent tens of thousands of dollars and thousands of hours trying to get new business. It became an obsession. But the answer was staring me in the face. I could get business through the people I already knew. I worked until I figured out how to build relationships on purpose and make my own luck. I'd like to teach you to do the same without the fear.

Despite my introversion, I'm a naturally gregarious person, and I like talking to people, so I probably had a head start. Once I figured out how to make touchpoints and follow up, however, the system took on a life of its own. Magic happened.

I went from struggling to pay the rent to now, years later, having a thriving business helping almost one hundred large companies per year solve their most serious business issues. We've grown 35 percent year over year for the last five years. We're on an exponential growth path, all thanks to relationship building, and I expect that trend to continue as long as I continue making connections to strengthen my network.

Just as importantly, however, I have a rich life full of people I enjoy. The phone rings, bringing me friends and experiences as well as work and interesting projects. I have the book of business I wanted in the beginning, and I have so much more besides. I've had the opportunity to meet wonderful employees, clients, friends, and buddies that I wouldn't have met otherwise. People built it all.

I want to help others connect to the richness I've found. Some of the guys who work with me have, naturally or otherwise, figured out how to do this. Others struggle. These are good people who want to take the next step in their careers but don't know how.

I wrote this book for them, in part, to show them—and you— how to do what I learned to do by necessity. Why not enrich your life with better relationships and build business at the same time? Why not enjoy what you do from nine to five in a new way? I like to help people, certainly, but sharing this system goes beyond altruism. If the people I work with and everyone else are able to make stronger connections, it helps me, too. We're all enriched when we make more connections.

A NOTE ON TERMS

When I say "guy" in this book, it's normally a shorthand for men, women, and transgender people. I've tried saying "guys and gals" or looking for a nongendered term, but I end up feeling cheesy. I've "got a gal" just doesn't have the right ring to it. "Guy" sounds better to me.

Forgive the fuzzy terms, please, and understand what I intend. "Guy" doesn't mean a male person in this book. It means a person you know. And we all need people we know who can help us.

WHAT TO EXPECT

This book is not sales training. It won't make the phone ring immediately or convince someone to sign on the dotted line if they aren't already ready. It also won't necessarily deliver for you in the first week—but the results compound. Nothing we're talking about is hard, though the system gets easier the more you do it. It's a lifestyle, not a diet.

Expect that you'll have to work at this for a while. Making your own luck is a habit you practice day after day, week after week. Talking to one person is great, but the real power happens when you talk to a hundred. You're putting yourself in the right place at the right time for when they need to call. You're chasing serendipity.

Ultimately, since this system is about genuine relationships, it becomes a lifestyle you can feel good about. You'll never have to be pushy, and people will be glad to see you when you reach out. People who hate hard sales can build great businesses using these techniques if they keep at it.

While building relationships is for everyone, this system won't help everyone equally well. A factory worker will get less out of the system than the person responsible for selling the cars the factory makes. The worker, however, might still benefit from strategic relationships as she works to be promoted to supervisor.

In other words, this book is for the people looking to advance their careers and their businesses. It is for everyone interacting with people every day.

THE LONGER YOU WORK, THE LUCKIER YOU GET

As I've already mentioned, you probably will get some results within the first few weeks, but the real power of this system happens as you keep doing it over time. Making one connection is great, but if you continue to create touchpoint after touchpoint, relationship after relationship, the results begin to compound.

Eventually, as Todd found out, you'll discover that people will send business your way because they liked you and they heard from you—even if only because your email got hacked.

Even a network of three thousand people, however, starts with one connection.

Let's talk about what it takes to build that one.

Chapter One

THIS IS REALLY SIMPLE

I was in the Philadelphia airport on the way back to Los Angeles when my iPad's charge died. I couldn't watch *The Wire*, and I wasn't hungry. I didn't want to go get a beer. So I opened up my phone and started randomly clicking through my contacts.

There she was! Georgia. I remembered Georgia—she'd worked with a former client. We had mutual contacts, and I remembered that she was an engaging lady. Even though we were on opposite sides of the table, even though we'd been a little acrimonious, there had always been a mutual respect. She was a worthy opponent. I liked her.

I wondered there in the airport why I hadn't stayed in touch with Georgia. I'd liked her. I should have stayed in touch. It was the kind of strange self-talk you have when you're bored. By then, however, I'd learned to do what I'm going to teach you in this book. I took that moment of boredom and I wrote an email.

In that email, I said something like, "Hi Georgia, it's been forever. I really meant to stay in touch. I hope you're doing well and everything stabilized after the last couple of years. I think good thoughts when I think of you."

Literally five minutes later she called me back. "Larry! Crazy world. I was just thinking of you. We need help on a project, and you guys would be perfect for it."

I got off the phone bemused. One email in a moment of boredom and suddenly I had a major new deal on my desk. Even for me, that was bizarre.

If I hadn't sent that email, it never would have happened.

OVERPREPARING THE POWERPOINT

Hugo is a brilliant guy who works for me. Everyone likes him, and he's great at his job. His one flaw is that he tends to fall into a project so deeply he forgets about the rest of the world.

Periodically, Hugo comes up for air to find that there's no more work to do. I call the phenomenon the sine curve effect.

If you only go looking for work when you're out of work, your work (and your sales efforts) ends up lumpy. Your world feels like feast or famine. A large percentage of people in professional services can end up with this kind of sine curve to their businesses. I've had to help Hugo, and dozens more, learn to maintain a practice to smooth over the curve.

In the beginning, when Hugo hit the famine stage, he spent two weeks putting together the best PowerPoint presentation he could possibly make. He spent hours of effort preparing to impress people with how great he and our firm were. Only then would he reach out to contacts.

Hugo, like so many other people I've talked to, lets the relationships go when he gets busy. Then, he spends excessive amounts of time preparing when it's time to reach out again. I believe that habit happens out of fear. Reaching out feels scary—I understand that. Waiting and overpreparing, however, just makes that fear worse.

TALK TO PEOPLE

To be clear, I'm not against PowerPoint. It's possible that some of Hugo's contacts found the PowerPoint he made useful. The bigger issue, however, is the opportunity cost. What else could Hugo have been doing with that two weeks?

He could have sent a lot of emails, for one.

Reaching out to a person on LinkedIn or email takes about three minutes. Reconnecting with old acquaintances often even feels easy. People you knew but have fallen out of touch with, like Georgia, are often people you liked. In two weeks, Hugo could have sent emails to every person he remembered fondly from the last ten years. He could have made his way through his college yearbook, LinkedIn, and the list of former colleagues and professionals he worked on projects with. He could have gotten started rewarming many relationships instead of reaching out to just one new one. Goodness knows, it's much harder to make a new friend than to say hello to an old one. Yet we all ignore the old ones to reach out to new.

I've been in business a long time now, and I can tell you definitively that warm relationships get you farther than all the razzle-dazzle PowerPoints in the world. You can't fake authentic, warm connections. A stranger may or may not listen to your presentation. A warm connection will always pick up the phone.

Even if you and the next guy both excel at what you do, your friend will still call you first because you're friends. A warm relationship starts with a three-minute message and continues with one lunch a quarter. It's easy to maintain, and highly effective. A warm relationship unlevels the playing field.

THE BAR IS LOW

Sometimes the things we think are easy end up being extremely difficult, and vice versa. Building relationships is one of those things. We think it'll be onerous—but it's actually simple.

So many hardworking people in my industry spend hours trying to find the perfect double backhand-flip to land the sale. In reality, business isn't complicated. People like to buy from people they like and trust. While they spend the two weeks on the PowerPoint, I'm out there talking with anyone who will listen. My approach goes farther.

You don't have to figure it all out. You don't have to get it perfect. You don't have to spend the hours on analysis paralysis or playing 3D chess with yourself. Instead, just reach out.

When you reach out, you get to have a pleasant interaction with a real human. When you stress about getting it perfect, you won't do it. As the old expression goes, you won't catch fish if your line isn't in the water.

If you only talked to one new person per week and kept up with them every few months consistently, you'd have fifty-two new relationships a year. Think of how absurd it is to talk with only one person per week! Building connections is much less onerous than you imagine.

SPIN THE WHEEL

How do you connect with people and stay in touch? I'll tell you in depth in chapters three and four, but for now, I'll go ahead and show you how simple it really is.

I open my phone and spin the wheel of my contacts. My eye lands on Victor—I remember him. We worked on a deal together two years ago. We keep in touch and have seen each other a few times. I like Victor and enjoy spending time with him.

What sticks out in my mind about Victor? What's the first thing that pops into my head? We had a dinner together where we were both on the same diet, and we got the steak with blue cheese on it. We'd chuckled together about how that was considered diet food.

Next, I'll write up a quick email to say hello and reconnect. "Hi Victor, it's been a long time. I don't know why I was thinking about this, but I remember that time we went to dinner and you ordered that 'diet' steak with blue cheese. Hope you're well. Let's catch up at some point."

The email doesn't have to be a big deal, and in fact it's better if it isn't. He'll likely get a chuckle out of the moment. We'll make a short human connection, and that'll be all it takes. It took three minutes, start to finish. No pitch. No awkwardness.

When you let someone know you're thinking of them, they feel good. They think of you in return. How do you feel when someone you haven't heard from in a while reaches out to you? You feel good, of course. To evoke the same response in someone else, you don't have to be dazzling—be human instead. Reach out and make a touchpoint just like the one I did.

DUNBAR'S NUMBER

Why do we create touchpoints and relationships with people? It's simple. We want to be top of mind. We want to make it into someone's Dunbar Number.

In *The Tipping Point,* Malcolm Gladwell explains an interesting idea that I love, originally conceptualized by British anthropologist Robin Dunbar. According to Dunbar, there's a limit to the group size that your neocortex can process individually.

Said another way, if you drop a few dozen pennies on the ground, your brain will be able to understand how many you see. Any number of pennies less than 150, and your brain will be able to estimate the amount reasonably accurately, within 10 to 20 percent. A number much bigger than 150—for example, 2,000—won't make the same sense to your brain. You won't be able to estimate how many there are with any degree of accuracy.

The theory, from a social anthropologist standpoint, is that humans evolved in social groups of about 150 individuals. In the plains, or wherever we started, 150 people was the right number. It's what we can conceptualize, and what makes sense to us emotionally. Too much larger, and we can't fully comprehend the number in a concrete way. It becomes abstract and intellectual rather than real and emotional.

Said more specifically, we as humans can only really keep track of about 150 people at a time.

HACKING DUNBAR'S NUMBER

The system I propose helps you become "top of mind." You don't have to be in the list of the five most important people in a person's life to be top of mind. You don't even have to make it into their top 150. You just have to be at the top of the list of, say, lawyers that they carry in their head. What's the expression about hiking and the bears? You don't have to be faster than the bear; you just have to be faster than your hiking partner.

I personally probably know three hundred lawyers. If someone asks me to recommend a lawyer, I'll page through my mental contacts list. I can't keep track of three hundred lawyers—my brain can't conceptualize the number. Instead, I think of my best friend, who's a lawyer, a second lawyer I had brisket sandwich with last week, and a third that I emailed yesterday.

The lunch and the email put those two lawyers at the top of my list. All three are great lawyers, but so is nearly every lawyer I know. The point is that I didn't spend the time to go through all three hundred lawyers in my life. I thought of those three, who I'd spent time with recently, confirmed mentally that they were great lawyers, and sent the introduction. Then I moved onto the rest of my day.

Strategic relationship building works because of the natural limits of human cognition. It works because of Dunbar's Number. If you're top of mind, you skip the line.

I work a little bit every week so I remain top of mind in other peoples' lives. I work to be a member of someone's mental small town, to be in their village, so they'll call me.

It has built my career.

A SIGN OF CONNECTION

"Networking" sounds intimidating...and, honestly, a little gross. I don't like the word. Instead, I like to focus on the word "touchpoint." Every touchpoint builds a piece of a bridge to a human connection, whether shallow or deep. A conversation with the barista at your coffee shop or hours spent on a project with a well-liked coworker both have value. Every interaction you have with another human being builds a connection, however fleeting. When we make those interactions on purpose, we call them touchpoints.

My six-year-old daughter's teacher taught her a sign of connection. She holds her hand in front of her with her pinky up and her thumb out, like a "hang loose" sign. If the teacher says something, or if someone in the class says something, that she connects with, my daughter will tap her thumb to her heart. I find that sign adorable; it so vividly illustrates the importance of connection.

Every time you reach out to someone, over email, in person, or with carrier pigeon, you connect with the person. She remembers that you're alive. You move to the top of her mind for a moment, in a positive association. You matter. If she needs your services that week, she'll call you first.

Touchpoints are the building blocks to connection.

A RANDOM CONNECTION

My friend Adam struck up a conversation with a stranger on an airplane. Over a long flight, they talked about their lives, their families, and their businesses. At the end of the flight, they'd had such a good time during the conversation that they exchanged emails. They'd connected on a human level and hoped it wasn't the last time they'd talk.

The person emailed Adam later, and they set up a time to meet for coffee and kept in touch. Randomly, then, over a year later she reached out. "Listen," she said, "I know this is coming out of thin air, but I think you said you worked on similar projects. My business partner is a quasi-investor. I wanted to run this past you just to see if you'd be interested or you think it's nonsense."

Adam got the details from her and got excited. "This project is brilliant," he told her. "I want to invest." He did, and in a short time got twenty times his investment back on the deal. I'll say it again, because it's so shocking: he got twenty times return from a deal he heard about from a random person on an airplane.

Every conversation that you enjoy is inherently valuable. Connecting with people is human, and worthwhile, all by itself. Every now and then, however, it'll turn into an amazing opportunity. If you can make twenty times your investment a few times in your life, you'll have done well.

Why not roll the dice and keep in touch?

WHAT TO TALK ABOUT

To connect with people, in person or online, you'll need to talk. What should you talk about? I'll give you an important hint. Don't feel like you have to talk about business. It's usually boring.

Talk about a book, or a vacation. Talk about pets, or kids, sports, or the latest *Game of Thrones* episode. Talk about something that a human being can relate to.

People don't care about how well I did in the last deal or how I won a turnaround of the year. No one gives a shit about that. They want to talk about their lives. They want to make connections. They need to feel heard.

If you can remember that someone's cat was sick and ask about the cat, you're in. You've made your way much higher up someone's intimacy spectrum. They feel close to you. You make them feel good, and their feeling good makes you feel good. It's a virtuous cycle. Taking the time to ask about someone's cat matters.

Don't worry too much about remembering the details if that's hard for you. Remember instead what you connected over. What mattered to you? How can you talk about that connection later in a light way that makes someone smile?

It's perfectly acceptable to say, "I remember having a great conversation. That was fun. I'd love to reconnect at some point." If you don't remember the cat, or the business, often it's enough just to say you had a good time and you wished you'd stayed in touch. The point is to connect with people.

ALL RELATIONSHIPS MATTER

I feel like people have a bias against relationships that aren't deep. Just because a connection isn't fully formed, or is in fact shallow, doesn't mean it's not worthwhile. If I genuinely enjoy going out for burritos with a guy, I'm not using him. I don't have to be the best man at his wedding for it to be a meaningful interaction. Maybe I'll get a charge of energy from the lunch, or perhaps I can help him in his business or his life. Perhaps he can help me. There's nothing but positive gains from that interaction!

I feel passionately about the importance of these so-called shallow relationships. I've had arguments defending them. Precious few people are going to be bridesmaids at your wedding, and that's absolutely fine. At your funeral, however, wouldn't it be nice to have people showing up because they enjoyed going out for burritos with you?

THE OPPOSITE OF SUPERFICIAL

Some people dismiss light and friendly interactions as unimportant. I'd argue that they're critically important. When you ask about people's lives, you're putting good energy out into the universe. What's the downside? Is that connection superficial? Certainly, chitchatting with someone every day on the train about the weather or the local sports team isn't deep, but the conversation is friendly and often heartfelt. It improves both your lives.

In studies, researchers have found that seniors who have regular human contact—the chats on the train, the conversations with the baristas or cashiers in their lives—live longer and in better health than those who are highly isolated.

Even small interactions—going for walks and seeing somebody, smiling at a child, talking about the weather with a friendly cashier—are important and human. I believe that every human interaction brings you alive in a small way. Dismissing these as superficial is shortsighted; every interaction has inherent value. Every friendly interaction—no matter how seemingly superficial—makes our lives richer.

Sometimes people (especially very junior people) don't reach out because they worry they won't be able to provide enough value to justify taking up someone else's time. Whenever I hear that worry, I get peeved and push back. "Is someone smiling for five minutes? Is that not valuable?"

Relationships shouldn't be transactional, even strategic ones. I'm not going to sell more consulting services because I made one more call today. Or at least, I certainly won't if that's my attitude. Instead, I'm focused on making this person's day just that much better, and perhaps reminding them that I'm alive, they like me, and I like them.

The value you're creating for people is a human connection, even if it's a momentary shallow one. If you can take someone scowling on the elevator and help them talk instead about the cat that they love, why wouldn't you? If you can take a moment to connect over family and distract someone from worry about their mortgage, why not?

Smiles are free, but not necessarily abundant. Smiles matter. The value is in the moments you get to be human.

MAKING ADVOCATES

Another major reason we increase our network and build relationships is to create advocates for ourselves in the world.

I'm a big believer in public relations rather than advertising. If I run an ad telling everyone how great I am, that's one thing. If the *New York Times* quotes me with the words "Larry Perkins, an expert in retail restructuring," suddenly the *New York Times* and its three-hundred-year history stands behind me.

A PowerPoint or a well-written white paper still feels like an ad. It's you telling everyone directly how smart you are. Building a network of people who like and trust you, in contrast, is like being quoted in *the New York Times*. Your advocates will lend you their credibility. They'll mention how great you are to their friends. They'll leverage their networks on your behalf.

An advocate will talk to her brother-in-law who works at a company that's in trouble. She'll say, "You know what? I met this interesting guy who helps companies turn situations around. You should call him." She'll mention you because you've made a connection and proven your value, and her brother-in-law will listen because he trusts her.

Building relationships through touchpoints is one of the most effective long-term business strategies that exists, because it leverages the power of people's trust. It creates advocates for you.

Make fewer ads and more advocates. They will bring more and better business to your firm.

A THOUSAND BUDDIES

When I talk about strategic relationship building, sometimes people worry that if they follow my advice, they won't be able to keep up with all the people in their lives. Not all relationships have to be deep ones, however.

I have fewer than ten very close friends, but I have a thousand buddies. Most of those buddies could likely become friends, given enough time and investment. I'm a human being with a long list of commitments, however, which tends to limit the depth in practice. That doesn't mean the relationship isn't an enjoyable one, but it does mean there are limits. I don't call my buddy when I'm getting bailed out of jail. I do enjoy getting burritos with him every few months.

RELATIONSHIPS MAKE THE BOSS HAPPY

Strategic relationship building also grows careers within companies. When you can bring in more business than it takes to keep yourself busy, you're directly growing the organization. You become valuable in a new way.

Any business bigger than a sole proprietor works by using leverage. Put another way, there are always people working for other people. When you bring in business, recruit friends, create strategic alliances, or otherwise help people through the relationships you build, you help the company. You create work for others, and you become infinitely more valuable to the organization. The contributions you make keep entire teams busy—and that means, sooner or later, you'll end up a leader of teams.

You don't have to deliver results right away to be valuable, however. Even as you're growing your network, you can connect people and be helpful. Your boss will want you in the room, even before you bring in major business, if you can help her socially. If you're the guy who knows where to take the big boss to dinner when he's in town, your boss will remember you at promotion season. Careers are made of such inane, helpful moments.

BEING THE BURRITO GUY

At my first job, I worked in an accounting firm on the consulting side. Forty people started at my level about the same time. Realistically, on paper, I ranked thirty-eighth out of forty in terms of grade point average and academic prowess. Everyone there seemed smarter than me by the book.

When it came to the work, though, I was good. I hustled. I learned. I delivered good work. The reason I got staffed, though, the reason I got noticed and promoted, had nothing whatsoever to do with my good work. I pulled ahead because clients liked me.

Just as importantly, however, while all the other twenty-one-year-olds were shy and quiet, I figured out where to get the best burritos in town. I became the guy you talked to when you wanted to find good food. In the end, when it came down to choosing me or Clarice, who was very good at balancing T-accounts but very bad at finding burritos, often the client would ask for me. They knew I'd show up with good lunches.

My actions weren't brown-nosey; they felt authentic, and so people liked me.

When my boss would call the clients at promotion time, the client would always ask, "Hey, where's the kid? Where's the burrito guy? How's he doing? You should send him back next time!" The senior partner John, a fifty-year-old grizzled veteran, was hearing about me from the clients because of those burritos. They'd ignore thirty other people on the job to ask specifically for me, even though I was twenty-two at the time. Those burritos elevated my career faster than anything.

ADDING A LITTLE JOY

Everyone does work. We work to do the things we love out of life. What if you could incorporate more of those things into your daily work life? Food, human connection, fun times, talking—these are all very basic human things.

There are moments in time where our careers are exciting. Other times, it's fun to talk about your cat, or think about a burrito, or talk about where you want to go on vacation. When you're grinding away at work, there's a moment when you're walking to the restroom, and you can say, "Yo, man, what're you doing this weekend? You going to watch the game?" Filling the white space with little moments of human connection feels good.

When you look at the math, people don't stay at jobs for the money. They stay for the people. Business is the same. When you have a choice between having two people work with you, wouldn't you choose the one who makes you feel good? Wouldn't you choose the moment of connection on the way to the restroom, the great lunches, and the laughs about the cool things your kids did?

Wouldn't you enjoy being that guy for someone else just as much?

YOU CAN DO THIS

People think that adding value to an organization is all about skills, and going above and beyond on delivering on those skills. Being the best at Excel is certainly valid. Working long hours is also cogent. Sometimes, however, the equation is about more than just the work. You can be the burrito guy, or the gal who knows the right people, the person who can string tennis rackets, or the vacation guy or gal. Often that will get you further than all the long hours in the world.

Adding value can be, and should be, as much about being a good human as the work itself. You're improving someone's life in some capacity, whether inside or outside of your profession. Since you're there anyway, why not brighten someone's day?

You have everything you need to connect. You don't have to spend two weeks making PowerPoints trying to impress people. Reach out, show up, and be a good human. Seriously, this system really is as easy as opening up your phone.

Don't spend a lot of time thinking it through. As Richard Branson said, "Screw it, just do it."

Well...with one caveat.

Chapter Two

YOU CAN'T BE AN EMPTY SUIT

Sometimes I go out for sausages with Steve. He's a partner at a law firm. I met him at one of those interminable industry mixer events, chitchatting, complaining about the event and the lack of good food, and suddenly I asked him, "hey, man, want to go get a sausage or something like that?"

We walked over to the sausage place around the corner, laughing the whole way, and got a sausage and a beer. It was a fun night. We stay in touch, and we're friends. We have similar interests and a family about the same age. It's easy.

Steve and I get friends together and invite them to weird off-the-radar restaurants while pretending we're fine dining. We both think it's hilarious. And, of course, we go out to eat sausages because that's what we do.

Two weeks ago, I got a call out of the blue from a huge fund wanting to hire my company. A partner at Steve's firm had sent out a blast email to all the other partners in the thousand-person law firm. His client was looking for someone who does what I do. Steve's my sausage-eating friend, so he replied with my name.

The contract will be for about $600,000 dollars.

VIOLET THE DESIGNER

I was at a music industry event with my wife one night when I struck up a conversation with Violet, who happened to be seated at the same table as us. We did the garden variety small talk, what I did for a living, the book I'm writing (which you're holding), and then turned our attention to what she did.

Violet is an interior designer. She'd apprenticed for a big-name designer and then started her own practice. I had no idea whether to be impressed—whenever I hear about interior design I never know if someone is picking out furniture for people or selling real estate with staging. Still, I liked Violet a lot. When I got home I looked up her work.

Her website was phenomenal. The houses she puts together are resplendent. Her work stood out for all the right reasons, for great taste and beautiful surroundings.

I don't need an interior designer right now, but if a client ever asks me where to find one, I'll mention Violet. She's at the head of my short list of interior designers. If an opportunity comes up, I will call her, because she was not only memorable and charming but very, very good at her job.

YOU MUST HAVE SKILLS

The method I'm teaching you in this book is tried and true. It will get you in the room. However, if you can't deliver once you're in the room, you won't last very long.

When I was burrito guy, I was literally the most junior person on the project. The client would ask for people to come back. "Charlotte, Huck, and Sue, of course, you guys need to be running point, but also make sure burrito guy comes out." They forgot about the other twenty-three people in between. If I hadn't been able to do the work, that wouldn't have happened. I would have been memorable as a joke, not a pleasant interaction.

If you're an entertainer, be memorable, but entertain. If you're an accountant, do accounting well. If you're a lawyer, you must know how to practice law, and the same for financial planning or anything else. What good is a pizza guy who can't deliver a pizza? He might be the most charming person you've ever met, but if he can't show up with the pizza, you won't call him.

You must have basic excellence in what you do. And excellence isn't too strong a word. I mean it. Have the highest standards for yourself, as that's effectively your advertising once you get in the door. If you can connect people and deliver socially or business-wise for people, do that. You'll elevate yourself beyond your native competency. But you must have that native competency to begin with.

Be memorable. Make people like you. Keep in mind, however, that you must also do the work well.

THE NETWORK EFFECT CAN WORK AGAINST YOU

I had a recruiting firm connect with me because the salesman had gone to the same college I went to. On paper, this firm was a perfect fit for what I do, so I took the meeting. I regret that decision.

When the salesman showed up at the meeting, he talked about football and stories from college, attempting to pull at my heartstrings. When it came time to do his presentation, however, it was obvious he didn't know my business. Worse, he didn't know the industry or any relevant things about how people get hired in our industry. In fact, he was so ill-prepared and seemingly incompetent that I was pissed off.

He'd been far more high-pressure than I'm comfortable with in the first place, but I'd taken the meeting. I'd started it with fondness because of the connection to my old college, but I ended that meeting with a bad taste in my mouth. I still think poorly of him, and I think poorly of his entire organization as a result.

Six months later, I got a call from someone who wanted to merge our business with a recruiting firm. When they told me the name of the firm, it was the same one that salesman had ruined for me. I told the caller that story, and they apologized for bringing it up. If I'd ever have been willing to do a deal with that firm, I certainly wasn't now.

The salesman did worse for his business that day than he would have calling in sick.

THE EMPTY SUIT

Failure happens. I've been in thousands of meetings with unsatisfactory outcomes. I've been to very few meetings where I—or the other party—was as actively bad as this recruiting firm was bad. Show up and do your work with care, and people will forgive a lot. Show up unprepared, and you'll leave a rotten taste in their mouths—and they will hold it against you.

That salesman was pushy, and he played on specious connections. He looked great on the outside. The company was an internet darling, with a great website full of beautiful people you just wanted to hire. When he showed up as unqualified, uninteresting, unprepared, and a series of every other "un" you can think of, I couldn't believe it was the same company. I didn't believe they could deliver what they said they could deliver. It felt like a lie.

The worst thing you can ever be is an empty suit.

BE WORTHY OF REFERRALS

In the same way that doing a great job for people will make them your advocates, doing a poor job for people will make them tell the story of your incompetency.

Someone is vouching for you every time you get a referral. Do work that's worthy of that referral. Make yourself look good and make the other person look good. Deliver great work. Build advocates, not detractors. Create friends, not enemies.

If you're going to be a DJ, be good at DJing a party. If you're going to be an accountant, be good at accounting. Skills don't happen by accident; they require practice and constant dedication. This system will get you in the room, but it won't deliver for your clients.

If you do everything I tell you to do, and then you walk into the meeting like that salesman walked into mine, you're doing yourself a disservice. You can be infinitely charming, and a good person, but if you almost went to law school, you won't be able to represent them in court. You'll make a fool out of both yourself and the person who recommended you.

So don't be an empty suit. Work your ass off to be worthy of the referrals.

CHECK WITH YOUR NETWORK

Similarly, don't work with people who are empty suits. As much as possible, screen people through your network of referrals in turn.

My company has a website and we do social media. Occasionally I'll get calls from those venues. I don't want to be too cynical, but it's a fact that the only two times I've done business with crooks, they came through the website from outside my network.

I probably get thirty-five emails a day from salespeople telling me how they're the greatest thing since sliced bread. I delete every one. When I need to hire someone to do a service for me, I don't Google unless I have no other choice. I first call around and ask for a referral. A network doesn't just come in handy for when it's time to help other people. A network surrounds you with people that other people vouch for.

On the other end, at the time of this writing, I was planning an event for the next year with a summer camp theme. I wanted to find a camp counselor who could lead games, pin the tail on the donkey, and whatever else you do at summer camp. Literally no one I know does that or knows anyone who does that.

I Googled, and found the name of a guy who does exactly what I wanted. I called him and asked for references. If he couldn't give me references, I would have known he was bullshitting me, but as it was he sent me two company references that checked out.

The camp counselor guy isn't an empty suit. I know because I found people who vouch for him.

DELIVER VALUE

Rather than focusing on yourself and what you can gain from a relationship, consider what value you can provide to your clients and coworkers.

What is value? In the context of services or goods, value means something I can't innately provide myself. If I'm hungry, pizza is super valuable. If I've been given an unjust parking ticket, legal services are valuable. If I need to go on vacation, having a friend who can tell me the best places to go on vacation may be incredibly valuable to me at that moment.

Look for opportunities to provide value to people, both within and without your profession. Pay attention to what they need. Deliver professionally and do an excellent job.

Not all value you *could* deliver, however, is value you *should* deliver.

KNOW YOUR LIMITS

If you aren't a lawyer, you can't deliver legal services. If you're a bad lawyer, and you deliver bad legal services, you won't make it. That part is hopefully obvious. However, not being an empty suit goes beyond hitting basic competency at your job. It also means knowing your limits and being willing to say no even in situations where that might feel tough.

If you're an intellectual property lawyer, you might establish a great relationship with ABC Company doing intellectual property work. If the CEO calls you out of the blue one day and says he's stolen a million dollars, you shouldn't represent him in a criminal case. That's not what you do. Overstepping your limits would get everyone in trouble.

However, referring the CEO to the criminal defense partner in your firm still makes you look like a hero. You'll have helped your client and given your criminal defense lawyer buddy some business. Both will remember you fondly because you will have helped both.

Have the integrity to deliver, and to say no when you can't. People may be annoyed at first, but will respect you more in the long run.

STAY ON YOUR LEVEL

If you do everything right to develop relationships perfectly and strategically, you can still mess it up if you ask for the wrong thing.

A guy used to work for us—let's call him Jack. He was very good at developing relationships and being memorable. What do I mean? As a junior guy, Jack managed to network his way into a meeting with a senior executive at a major bank. They bonded over surfing and jazz.

Jack set up the meeting for himself. He went to the headquarters of the big national bank and sat there for twenty minutes talking about surfing and jazz. Finally, the executive asked him what the meeting was about, and Jack froze. By the time he stammered a half-hearted sales pitch, it was all over. The executive was irritated he'd wasted time on a Thursday. I think the executive admired what Jack was doing, so it wasn't a catastrophe, but I, as Jack's boss, had to call personally to smooth things over.

Jack shouldn't have been trying to sell to someone at that level. Some things are best accomplished peer to peer. Jack didn't have the standing to speak to the executive's needs or to help him effectively with connections.

Had it been a pure social introduction, Jack might have been able to pull off, but as it stood, it just ended up being an awkward, coachable moment for Jack.

WHAT YOU CAN ACTUALLY DELIVER

What did Jack do wrong? He was a different kind of empty suit. He did good work, but he didn't have the other intangibles to back up what he was promising through his actions.

Jack did an unbelievable job getting into that room—that took genius-level social skills. Where he fell down was not enlisting his bosses or colleagues to go with him to the meeting. The executive would have benefited more from the meeting, the colleagues would have had a legitimate shot, and Jack would have looked like a hero for pulling it together. A rare win-win,-win. But Jack swung for the fences on his own and got beyond what he could deliver.

Be thoughtful about your role and what you're trying to do (and can do) at your present career level. In the beginning, you'll likely be focused on simply expanding your network. Good things happen to those with large networks. If you happen to come across an opportunity, pass it up the chain to your boss.

As you get more senior, you might transition into making the sale yourself. Then, at an even more senior level, you'll move into trying to get someone a board seat or get your kid into school. At a certain level, you often get one ask. Make sure that you spend it on the thing you really need. Don't overshoot what you have the credit to accomplish.

To make it into the room with the VP effectively, you'll need the social capital to be able to offer him value in return. Make sure that you have that capital before you show up, or you'll frustrate everyone in the process.

ESCHEW SHOWINESS

We've all seen the salesperson trying to be impressive. We've all seen that person who puffs up their credentials, or who won't stop talking about their latest self-aggrandizing accomplishment. Over time, I stop listening. No one likes to be razzle-dazzled.

In contrast, when I'm in a conversation with a nice person, sometimes I'll find—as I did in the conversation with Violet— that the person is even more accomplished and interesting than I'd realized. There's nothing so fun as being pleasantly surprised.

When the person walks in saying how great they are, at best, they're on par with what they've told me and often they're considerably less. When I walk in without an expectation and discover greatness, however, I walk away singing.

We've all been there. We sit down on a park bench and talk to someone feeding the pigeons, and it turns out they used to be mayor. Or we talk to a guy on an airplane for forty minutes before it comes out he manages four manufacturing plants.

Don't be showy. Instead, let your greatness come out naturally in its own time. Humility gives people a chance to be surprised by you, and surprise is charming.

MOVING ON

I'm guessing that this chapter is largely irrelevant to you, because you're not an empty suit. You're great at your job, and you continue to work to stay great at your job. So let's move on to figuring out how to elevate your greatness through strategic relationship building.

How do you build your network? Make connections, reach out, and do the thing I call communing. Be part of a community, stay engaged in peoples' lives, and help. Relationships are not trophies on the wall. They're things you actively engage with on a regular basis.

Let's get into the nitty-gritty.

Chapter Three

===============

THE NITTY-GRITTY

I have a theory about grilled cheese sandwiches. The recipe has three ingredients: butter, cheese, and bread. Anyone can make it. Having a truly outstanding grilled cheese sandwich, therefore, becomes entirely about applying intention and skill.

Because greatness in grilled cheese is entirely about the execution, having a great sandwich becomes a transformative event. You can go to a restaurant and get a dish with two dozen ingredients and be less impressed than you would be with a truly exceptional grilled cheese sandwich. Or at least, that's my theory. The popularity of seventeen-dollar artisan versions at restaurants—and Instagram channels dedicated to the topic—would seem to support my theory.

Building relationships is like making grilled cheese sandwiches. The recipe is simple. Being just a little more intentional about that process, however, can be the difference between an acceptable grilled cheese you threw in the microwave and one that brings tears to your eyes. Everyone can make grilled cheese. If you prepare carefully, get the cast iron pan out, and use the butter, you can make a great sandwich. There's nothing hard here. However, a great grilled cheese doesn't happen by accident. It takes thoughtful preparation and execution to deliver a great result.

If you're building relationships anyway, why not learn to do them well? In other words, why create a mediocre sandwich when you can craft a damn good grilled cheese?

YOU'RE ALREADY GOOD AT THIS

Every day of your life, you talk to someone. Many of them you already have some sort of relationship with. Becoming top of mind to more people means extending the way of life you already have.

When I've talked about this system, many people start tensing up. Reaching out to people doesn't have to be frightening! We're not talking about sticking out your hand to a stranger that you've never met. Quite the contrary. Talking to people is one of the most prosaic, natural activities in your life—something you do, day in and day out, already. What we're talking about in this book is doing it on purpose.

If you're reluctant to talk to people, or have anxiety about talking to people, it's often freeing to discover how many people you already talk to on a regular basis. So let's go through a quick inventory.

Open up your phone and thumb through your contacts. Then, think for a moment about how you keep track of the people you know. Are they in your phone, in Outlook, in an old school Filofax or notebook, or mostly in LinkedIn? Who do you see and talk to habitually? Who did you see and talk to in the past? Wherever you keep your list—and expect that you'll probably keep them in several places, some only in your head—take a minute and literally look through the people in your life.

Whether you have hundreds of names on your list or a dozen people you appreciate greatly, seeing the names in black and white can be invigorating. You'll see people that you remember from school. You'll see people you used to work with, or do CrossFit with. Whatever. You're already social. You're already talking to people. You already have everything you need.

We all have people we want to be in our lives, whether that's because we like them or perhaps because we think they can help us in our pursuits. In a perfect world it's both. Being around people who we like and can help (and get help from) is human. Learning to connect with people intentionally is just the next level up from something you're already good at.

Becoming top of mind with the people you want is about making them think of you in a positive way. How do you do that? We'll go into detailed specifics throughout this "how to" chapter, but in its most simple form this system is about connecting. Talk about what you're doing and they're doing. Reconnect. See if you can either engage further in a relationship you already have, or reengage a relationship that may have fallen off.

To do that, we'll need to engage with your contacts list.

TAKE A MINUTE TO CLEAN UP

Your contact list (however you keep it/them) will be the engine of your system. You'll use it daily and weekly as a tool to create touchpoints with the people you want in your life. Because of the ubiquity of using that list, I'd recommend you spend a little time periodically cleaning it up. If you have someone you don't want to talk to any more (maybe an ex-girlfriend or -boyfriend, for example), go ahead and delete them. Your contacts list should be a place you go to feel good, not a messy place with complicated feelings.

As with so many other things, however, here I believe that perfect is the enemy of the good. Don't go down the rabbit hole, but do take a minute to clean up extraneous contacts as you go. The pizza place you used to order from three apartments ago doesn't belong in a list you'll need to use today.

Once you've got your contacts lists in good order, you're ready to make touchpoints.

WHAT IS A TOUCHPOINT?

Connecting with people happens naturally every day. Turning those connections into relationships, however, takes effort. It takes a little courage and vulnerability to follow up, and to put yourself out there.

Every time you reach out deliberately to connect, that's a touchpoint. Every phone call, text, email, or anything else you use to reach out and make a connection. (LinkedIn Messenger? Website contact page? Carrier pigeon? Whatever seems natural and nonthreatening. The sky's the limit.)

It may make sense to say what a touchpoint isn't. If you send a quasi-spam, impersonal, cookie-cutter message saying how great you or your company is, that's not a touchpoint. You may get attention, but you'll just as quickly get deleted. The one-to-one messages are far more likely to get a smile.

Touchpoints should spark a memory of the connection you made with that person, however deep or shallow. It's a brief touch that reminds you both you're interesting people and you like each other.

I call these moments touchpoints for a few reasons. I used

to call them touches, because they make people feel touched, but I found that the word wasn't communicating as well as I'd like. When I added the word "point," suddenly the concept felt as warm as I meant it to be and was certainly less creepy.

There's something very personal about reaching out and connecting with another human. For one moment, you've found your way into another human's brain in a positive way. You've had a point of contact across the cosmos, each thinking about the other for a brief second of time.

Touchpoints are often very brief messages. They are "Thinking of you," "Hope you are well," and "I remember that one time we got nachos and laughed about koi ponds." They are brief moments that build bridges between people.

PLEASANT CONNECTIONS

I see my wife every day, and we interact naturally dozens of times per day. That relationship happens without touchpoints. Touchpoints are also not for the colleague I see at the office every workday—that relationship evolves organically and isn't something I have to take special effort to develop.

Touchpoints should always be a pleasant experience for everyone, as milquetoast as that sounds. They should be light, happy, warm, ephemeral moments—one human being looking across the savanna at another human being knowing that they are not alone.

A touchpoint is not a spam message. It's not a pitch. It's certainly not a generic missive that you could send by the dozens—it's personal and heartfelt. You're not asking; you're giving. You're not demanding; you're connecting. You're offering a cozy hello.

Recently I was at a farmer's market on a Sunday, buying my artisan almond butter, when I happened to be in line with someone I played flag football with twenty-five years ago. Suddenly I remembered a funny story about him and told it to him. He could not believe I remembered the story! We both had such good feelings reconnecting. He had a son the same age as my daughter, and we vowed to get back together. That was probably the best part of my day. Creating touchpoints means making those moments for other people deliberately, whether in person or virtually. Touchpoints create nice, cozy moments of connection.

Reaching out, particularly when you're new at the practice, can feel a little vulnerable. You fear you're going to be rejected, but that fear isn't warranted. I've probably reached out to create five thousand touchpoints over my career. Maybe once in all that time has someone responded with rejection. That was a rare breed of asshole. Most people are touched when you reach out. They think it's cool that you thought of them, even if it was only for twenty seconds. They're honored.

Touchpoints create communities. They build bridges, and ultimately they build networks. They're foundation points that allow you to help people and to be helped in return. Touchpoints feel good.

AN OPPORTUNITY TO RECONNECT

How do you choose who to reach out to? I like to focus on the people I liked and haven't talked to in a while.

Go through your contact list (on your phone, email, and anywhere else) and see if there's anyone whose name makes you smile. Often I'll run into a name and have a pleasant memory. Wait, I remember that person. It's been a long time, but I liked them and had a great time talking to them.

Think about that person. What did you guys do or talk about? Were you college friends? Work colleagues? Did you have a pleasant lunch or interaction at a conference years ago? Try to remember something about the person, whether it's the name of their dog or an interesting project they were working on at the office. If you enjoyed the interaction, often that will make it easier.

As we talked about in the example earlier in the book, including a small detail in your touchpoint lets the person know you're thinking about them as a human, not a commodity or somebody you're trying to mine. Small details let you connect.

PAY ATTENTION

Sometimes people are afraid they won't remember details, but I challenge you to spend time with someone and remember nothing about them whatsoever.

If you connect on an emotional level with someone, you enjoy a laugh, a conversation, or a meal, that's a worthwhile human interaction. If you pay attention, something about it will stick out.

Perhaps you spend time with a woman who has a cat named Waffles. The next time you see her in person or reach out with a touchpoint, ask about Waffles. She will be charmed you remembered. Even if you don't remember the cat's name, however, just mentioning her cat will earn goodwill.

Email remembers everything! Don't be afraid to search your inbox for your last interaction with someone. Particularly for the people you email infrequently, having a record of the last conversation can be freeing. You can email a detail to yourself if you want to be reminded when next you search for that person's name. Or you can make a note in your phone's notes section under the contact card for the person.

That being said, I have over three thousand contacts that I keep up with infrequently. I rarely need notes. Once I see someone's name, details come up. I'm guessing, if you pay attention to people, you'll find the same will happen for you.

AUTHENTICITY

Touchpoints can't be generic one-size-fits-all messages. You can't look someone up on a list of CEOs of companies in Los Angeles and send a generic message out of the blue. You also can't get your assistant or artificially intelligent robot to send a list of messages and expect them to have nearly the same impact.

Touchpoints work when they tap into authentic human connections. When someone reaches out to me well, I think that he actually remembers me, and we were actually at that event, breathing the same air, for a period of time. He's not trying to just "get to me." There was a connection there, however slight, that feels human, and he, himself, followed up on it. Even though that person may be reaching out primarily for business, the goal was accomplished. I remember he's alive and I think of him.

Keep in mind that meeting someone for thirty seconds doesn't give you the right to talk to them a week later. It's not enough to have gotten someone's business card at a mixer. Having a name on a piece of paper is not a connection. Having had a conversation about the very bad coffee or laughing about someone's special way of making coffee in a French press might be.

Ideally, you'll be following up with people you think are interesting, or that you like, even if it's in a very cursory way. These are people you'll have had conversations with. You wanted to follow up with them.

Reaching out with a touchpoint should be a natural extension of a connection you already made.

AN EXAMPLE TOUCHPOINT

Here's an example of a good touchpoint you might send over email.

Hi [Name],

It's been too long. I remember that time when we had lunch, and were talking about your daughter being afraid of the tooth fairy. My daughter has now lost three teeth and is squarely in the pro-tooth fairy camp. Whatever happened with that?

Hope you're doing well. It'd be great to catch up soon.

Larry

The email is fifty-seven words. It takes less than two minutes to write and send—perhaps five minutes if you need some time to think about the right detail. For the price of a handful of minutes, you can shoot a rocket into the universe to let someone know you're thinking about them.

When the person opens the email, they'll get a happy warm feeling. You'll be at the top of their mind for a moment. If they happen to have a need for your services, they'll call you, but more importantly, they'll think fondly of you in the meantime.

Touchpoints aren't hard.

THE FOLLOW-UP TOUCHPOINT

Here are another few examples of touchpoints for other common situations.

Let's say I had lunch with someone three weeks ago and just failed to follow up. I'd write an email like the following one:

I know we had a lunch three weeks ago, and we had a hundred different things to follow up with. I didn't do any of them, shame on me. Let's catch up on the phone sometime soon so we can figure out what to do.

If it's a friend that you saw at your high school reunion a year ago, and you happen to have their cell phone, a text might be appropriate.

Scout, for some reason I was thinking about you and that dance at the high school gymnasium. Crazy, huh? Hope you're doing well. We should catch up soon.

If I bumped into someone at a community event and said I'd give them a call, I'll call them when I remember, whether that's a few days later or a few weeks.

CHOOSING THE RIGHT TOUCHPOINT

Part of being a good human is paying attention to the person you've met and the context. A woman you met at your daughter's school might best be approached with a quick text. An interesting lawyer from a formal business meeting might need a thank you note or email "hello." Keep it light and simple, and exactly as formal as needed.

I like to think of different kinds of contact like different rungs on a ladder of formality. On the top of the ladder sits the most formal contact method, handwritten thank you notes. I used to send thank you notes all the time. Literally probably thousands of them. But I found that—though many people loved the notes—the ones who didn't felt that I was trying too hard.

Being too formal can land badly! On the other hand, in the

right context, formal can be charming. You'll know based on your conversation with the person and how casual your surroundings were or were not at the time. Sometimes you'll misjudge, and that's okay, too.

One next rung down the formality ladder is email. Email is the workhorse of business communication and rarely goes wrong. I might be a little old-school for thinking most business touchpoints should go through email, though—I've seen guys in my company make great business connections with everything from LinkedIn to text. The point is that it should feel natural to the recipient. If your recipient is forty-two—like me—or older, stick with email. Otherwise, use what seems natural to you and the person you're connecting to.

I'd place social media messages as less formal than email but less personal than text. I've reached out many times to friends and buddies on LinkedIn, saying I'd seen a post of theirs, their work anniversary, or big announcement and hoped they were doing well. I'll talk about my approach to these messages in a moment, but the point is that social media can feel personal and appropriate even for business purposes, if you personalize the message.

Text and phone calls sit on the bottom rung of the ladder, least formal and most warm—or intrusive if you overstep. The right person can find a phone call charming even in a business context, but it's unusual. In 2019, I feel like we're all constantly on the run, and a text often requires less effort than talking while giving someone your full attention. I'd suggest being careful with the phone unless you know it will land well or you know you really are friends. Occasionally an acquaintance will call me to chitchat—and I personally am glad to hear from them—but it always feels weird. Text is becoming more standard than phone calls. You might say, "Hey man, been too long. Give me a call when you get a second to catch up. Not urgent, just miss you."

In case it's not obvious, if it's been a long time since you've last talked, use the communication method you last used. If you texted six months ago, text now. If you called two years ago, however, you might text to set up a time to call now. Use as much warmth as possible without getting overly personal. Also, be mindful of the other person's preferences. If someone says, I don't check emails, or I hate talking on the phone, it's a *subtle* clue.

If it's been a while since you've last talked, that doesn't mean you're out of luck. I've been known to follow up with someone literally years later. "Hey there. We had lunch together three years ago, and I absolutely meant to follow up. I put on a coat I hadn't worn since then, and the receipt from that lunch was in the pocket. Two things: one, I should get the coat cleaned more; and two, I'm finally following up, and hope you're well." For the most part that gets a chuckle, and sometimes the person will suggest we do lunch again.

Even though I'm not exceptionally memorable, I've done this hundreds of times. People virtually always remember me if I prompt them. Maybe they don't remember as much as I do, and maybe they don't want to reconnect, but I reach out knowing it will nearly always land well.

EMAIL REMEMBERS SO YOU DON'T HAVE TO

If you go through your inbox from a few years ago, you'll find people you haven't talked to since that time. Often you'll find the conversation exactly where you left off! Who did you enjoy a few years ago? Who is someone you should reach out to now?

I've been known to reply to emails from three years ago for a laugh. If the last email was "Hey do you want to get lunch on Thursday?" I'll reply "I think I missed that lunch. I'm picking this back up—how about next Thursday?" Whoever I'm emailing usually chuckles and finds a time for lunch. When you go back in time into the archives, you'll be surprised at the gems that pop up.

MAKE SOCIAL MEDIA PERSONAL

I suggest that if you use LinkedIn or other social media for business that you don't use the prepackaged suggested messages. Instead, take the seventeen nanoseconds to personalize. Make the message feel personal and cozy, or risk coming across as lazy.

Every year on my birthday, I get hundreds of identical thank you notes. The LinkedIn AI suggested that the people send me a happy birthday message—all well and good—but hundreds of people then send the pre-programmed message. The message actually backfires, coming across as negative to me. I feel like they didn't spend the ninety seconds it would take to be personal. I'm irritated that I meant so little to them.

I accept almost anyone as a contact on LinkedIn, with the exception of true scammers. The reason for that could fill up the sequel to this book. (Teaser!) So my LinkedIn page is only vaguely reflective of the people I know in real life. When someone takes the time to personalize a message, I'm charmed. They shoot to the top of the pack.

DON'T LET THE RELATIONSHIP GET COLD

At one point I worked directly for a woman named Dominique. We did a great job for her company, we'd built tremendous credibility, and she was in a good position for my industry. I should have stayed in touch but for whatever reason failed to do so. (I screwed up. It happens.)

Now, if I reach out to her, I'll have to remind her who I am and recap the last five years. I might actually need a razzle-dazzle PowerPoint. It's far easier, in contrast, if I had spent five minutes once per quarter (and perhaps a lunch a quarter or per year) staying in touch. Rather than eighty hours, I'd have gotten the same yield from eighty minutes done consistently in five- and ten-minute increments.

Sometimes you can't rekindle an old relationship if it's gotten too cold. For relationships that were more transactional, like an accounting firm that you hired years ago, if the firm wasn't memorable, you won't necessarily give them more business just because they called you after five years.

If Dominique likes her new consulting firm and I've let the relationship go, my name might mean little to her—now. If I'd followed up consistently, perhaps I might have been the person she hired that second time. Now it's too late.

Don't be a stranger...Stay in touch.

CONSISTENCY MATTERS

Remember Hugo from my office, who spent two weeks making PowerPoints? I told that story partially to bring up what I call the sine curve. It's very common in professional services for people to have more work than they can handle, and then the work dries up and they go looking for more.

When Hugo went hot and heavy on networking and calling people, he got meetings, and he got business from the meetings. Then he stopped networking for nine months while he digested the business he got. The result was that people were always surprised to hear from Hugo when he did reach out.

I've heard from close friends that they appreciate my being consistent. They juxtapose my approach against a competitor in my industry who only calls when he needs something. His infrequent faux-collegiality doesn't ring true, whereas my steady follow-ups feel authentic. The warmth and consistency gives me an advantage.

Letting relationships go cold and then pursuing them is never as effective as keeping the relationship warm in the first place. Also, if you want your business to arrive with some regularity, you'll need to reach out regularly. Otherwise you end up contributing to your own feast or famine cycle.

It's far more effective to keep the relationships going at a steady pace, and reap the rewards more steadily. Prioritize a reasonable number of touchpoints every week, and your sine curve will flatten out. One is better than none. Ten is better than five. Thirty is better than twenty. Be consistent.

REMEMBERING TO REACH OUT

I've emphasized that creating touchpoints isn't as useful if you only do it once per year. So, then, how often should you reach out? Do you need to set reminders on your calendar?

For a while I actually did put scheduled reminders on my calendar to remind me to reach out. I'd keep a list of the thirty people I reached out to that week, and remind myself to check in with them again in about three months. I don't have to do that anymore, because I've found the rhythm of my life naturally lends itself to touchpoints and I tend to follow up often enough to keep most relationships warm naturally. It also starts happening for you, as people will reach out as part of their communication pattern. As long as I focus on talking to thirty people every week, the rest sorts itself out. You'll have to find what system and number works for you.

You may not want to talk to thirty people every week—you might want to do ten touchpoints. Life will happen, and you'll get reminded of at least five or six people naturally. When that happens, stop and reach out. Whatever you were thinking about provides a great topic to talk about in your message.

Think about your goals in terms of one-week sections. A month is too long—it feels intimidating. A week is just right. If you've been a hermit all week, you can wake up on Friday afternoon and knock out your touchpoints in ten to fifteen minutes. If you find you need to keep lists and reminders, do so. Do what works for you.

The most important thing is staying consistent. The longer you practice this system, the more people you'll be in contact with. You'll want to take more care to keep relationships warm over time. It's rarely too late for someone you were truly close to, but staying on top of your list makes a difference. Reinvigorating relationships that pooped out ten years ago is harder than breathing new life into a relationship with last month's lunch buddy. An acquaintance from ten years ago takes a lot more work to rekindle.

FOLLOWING UP

Not to be too obvious here, but the most important part about following up is, in fact, following up. That sounds trite, but it's true.

Following up seems intimidating for some reason. Simply remind people that you're alive, and you'll get much farther than trying to do it perfectly. Get on the phone. Send the email. Start with that humble goal, and actually do it. You'll get farther acting imperfectly than all the perfectionists in the world together doing nothing.

I had an interesting meeting with a provider of CRM software recently. The salesman said something sagacious. "Sometimes a note, any kind of note, is better than perfectly written prose. You could just write "telecom, dog food," and it will give you all the context in the world to restart the conversation later. If you don't make the note, though, you won't have the context."

Oftentimes follow-ups are very much like that note. You'll start a conversation, and a month later you'll continue it over lunch. Or you'll simply remind the person that you're alive, and start a new conversation. When you have the context, it's easy to resume the relationship. When you let it go too long, it becomes hard.

Follow up regularly.

NETWORKING EVENTS MATTER

Does anyone like networking events, really? Every industry has them, and in every industry, people like to stand around and complain about them. I personally hate the things. The food's bad, the drinks are bad, and you're on your feet for hours. I still go for one simple reason.

At every networking event, every conference, and every speaker event, I hope to meet two new people. If I can meet two people I like and want to follow up with, I consider the event successful. To get there, I have many three- to five-minute conversations and get many business cards. Without letting anyone see, I'll put a red dot in the corner of the ones I'll be following up with.

The next day, I'll send out touchpoint emails. Often they'll sound something like this. "John, nice meeting you last night. The event was pretty terrible, but you were a good guy. Would love to catch up for coffee or lunch at some point or whatever you'd like to do from there. I really enjoyed the conversation."

CONTINUING THE SYSTEM

Once you know how to do a touchpoint, what then? Every relationship has a natural progression through several distinct stages before I can arrive at a fully productive end state. In the next chapter, I'll walk you through the stages, what to expect, and how to grow your relationships to ones that will benefit both you and the other parties.

Chapter Four

THE FOUR PARTS OF THE BUSINESS CYCLE

My wife, Nichole, recently bid on an event at a preschool fundraiser's silent auction. She "won" the opportunity to go have tea and crumpets at someone's house and talk to the owner of a ballet company. It sounded like a fun thing to do with a daughter who is interested in all things pretty.

After the event, Nichole texted me, excited. She was having a great time, but our daughter, Dagny, had hit her limit and Nichole wanted me to come pick Dagny up so she could stay longer. No problem, I said, and drove down there.

That night, Nichole waxed poetic about Theresa, the co-founder of the ballet company. Theresa was apparently a beacon of brightness and light, and the company was amazing (which it absolutely is). Theresa had gotten

Nichole's cell phone number, and she followed up a few days later.

Theresa is extraordinarily good at the system I'm teaching you. They met for coffee, with Theresa telling Nichole about her dance background and how the company worked. We went to some of the company's performances, and they were amazing. Theresa is so charming and personable, in fact, that when it came time to do a corporate mixer where we highlight local artists, we invited her and a friend to the Salon.

Theresa, her co-founder Lincoln, and a troupe of the dancers showed up at the dinner, mingling and making friends. They had a blast, and more importantly, they got the names of a half dozen people who ended up becoming patrons of the ballet. A couple of them were even interested in sitting on the board.

Suddenly, as a result of very natural networking and connections, Theresa's ballet company has a lot more resources, including money to operate. They're expanding, and they're able to give more performances and do more experimental dance. In less than a year, she's landed a long list of motivated patrons simply by being charming and following up.

Inviting Theresa to our event helped her. The truth is that it helped me, too. Having a charming person who didn't talk about the same business all day long gave my Salon fresh energy. It made me look good to my friends. Art and dance are, in a way, frivolous and light. They're easy to talk about. But they're also important—they're part of the joy that makes life worth living.

While Theresa's story seemed linear to me, with one event leading to big results, from her perspective I have no doubt she had to kiss a lot of frogs. I've built relationships long enough to know that it takes time to find people who want to help—and have the ability. That's part of the game.

WHAT THERESA DID WELL

Theresa did many things well. To begin with, she put herself out there. She showed up at many events and mixers, culminating in the school fundraiser Nichole saw. She came up with a great idea for a tea and crumpets event. I have no doubt she was doing those sorts of activities for, possibly, years before she saw results.

Theresa was interesting and amiable. She introduced herself and was pleasant and charming to be around. She connected with the other human beings at every event she went to.

She did a great job following up with Nichole, to say she'd really enjoyed talking to her. "I'd like to figure out what your interests are, why you came, and talk a little more about what we're trying to do." The conversation felt like anything but a sales pitch, but Nichole ended the exchange knowing a lot about how the ballet ran and what it needed. She had a clear idea of how she could help.

Theresa encouraged us to buy tickets to witness her company in action. She greeted us warmly when we went. The ballet was cool, gritty, beautiful, creative, and so different than anything I see. I am anything but a ballet aficionado, but I was hooked. In other words, she was anything but an "empty suit."

When we approached Theresa to introduce her to more of our people, she jumped at the chance. She was such a good person that we wanted to help her, and she graciously accepted the help in a way that made us feel good. She delivered on our trust, and she followed up with people who became her patrons. Theresa did everything right.

Many people begin the process of strategic relationship building and get tired somewhere in the process. Perhaps they don't follow up, or perhaps they have an off night and don't connect with people at the events. Perhaps they don't explain their business well or accept help graciously. Realistically, Theresa probably had thirty or forty people to talk to at every stage of the process. She'd end with three to five who were truly interested. She could have messed up at any point.

However, Theresa did it right. She built relationships. She

made people like her, and over time, turned enough of those relationships into productive ones to grow her ballet. In turn, she helped all of us look good.

Given the right opportunity, I would absolutely invite Theresa to another event. The relationship was productive for us both.

MORE THAN TOUCHPOINTS

The system I'm teaching you is about more than just touchpoints. Meeting people and following up is essential but not sufficient. You have to grow relationships, too. Once you've connected, you'll have to move people through the business cycle to reach a productive relationship.

I'll pause and mention here that not everyone is a business contact. Friendships are worth pursuing for their own sake, and some relationships will be meaningful in arenas other than business—for example, parenting, or charity contacts. Inviting Theresa to my company mixer helped all of us have something to talk about beyond work, and that was valuable to me in a different way. For purely business contacts, however, you'll always go through several stages.

Be aware that you won't go for coffee once and be making large business deals. That's not how this works. You don't eat the elephant all at once. People build trust over time, and that's as true in this arena as any other.

I'll talk you through the stages of a business relationship and how to move from one to another. Then, we'll cover how to hack your way through the system so you don't always have to do every step.

STEP ONE: ESTABLISHING BONA FIDES

To create a business relationship, you'll first choose people to connect with. Not every person you meet will be someone you'll want to follow up with. I've definitely met people I don't want to talk to again, whether it's because I didn't like them or something about that interaction felt shady. There are many good reasons not to pursue a business relationship.

If, however, you meet someone you actually want to spend time with, great. You'll want to choose people who can be helpful to you and to whom you can be helpful in return. Not everyone has to be your best friend, but you do have to get along. It's even better if you enjoy spending time around the person.

Once you like the person, you'll create touchpoints and follow up like we've talked about. Establish rapport. Do a coffee, or a lunch. Have a conversation or three. You're establishing the early part of a pleasant relationship, however deep or shallow it becomes.

I think of this early stage as establishing *bona fides*. You're a nice person, I'm a nice person, we both like eating sandwiches, we both like looking at the moon. Once you've done that, it's time to move on to an early business conversation.

STEP TWO: ESTABLISHING WHAT YOU DO

Often, if you meet someone in a work context, he or she will already have some idea of what you do for a living. That's great. However, you'll still want to have this second conversation. We all give one-sentence answers at a cocktail party. True understanding takes a little longer.

I like to think of the second conversation as "Help me understand deeply what you do, what your organization does, and why we're here beyond the friendship side." Go out of your way to avoid sounding like a sales pitch, but do connect what you do to the other person's role. Start by seeking to understand the other person first.

Say I've been going to lunch with someone who works at a law firm. (I know a lot of lawyers, so it's an example I think of quickly.) I'd first ask what kind of lawyer the person is. "I'm an environmental lawyer." Great. Does that mean you're suing people to get money from environmental polluters, or are you defending companies from getting sued by people on the same issue?

Taking it a step further, is there a particular specialty you have within that field? Are you talking nuclear waste? Groundwater pollution? Something else? I try to get very curious and ask many questions to get inside someone's head.

If you're remotely interested in what someone does, this conversation can be very enjoyable for everyone. If you do a good job asking curious questions, people will often like you better afterward. Dale Carnegie said, "People love talking about themselves." You'll also get the benefit of hearing about someone's work more deeply.

Understanding How They Can Help

At some point in the conversation, hopefully the person will ask you questions. Be forthcoming and specific. Also, if you can, mention how your work can help someone like the person sitting in front of you.

How does this work? If someone asks me where I get my referrals from, I answer in a specific way. If I'm talking to a lawyer, I'll say, "We get referrals from banks, private equity firms, even boards of directors. I've even gotten referrals from my dentist. Honestly, we get a lot of referrals from lawyers. We often get referrals from law firms just like yours."

If you're clear with your intonation and phrasing, the point becomes clear. Suddenly the lawyer in front of me understands how she can help me. Often she'll follow up with questions. "When would a potential client call you? How do you work with clients once we've made the call?"

If what you do is particularly complex, be prepared to have the understanding conversation more than once. You may also need to have it more than once if the person talks about themselves the whole time the first time around. That's fine! If you're good at listening, you'll have learned something and built goodwill in the meantime. Do come back around to explaining what you do in turn.

Often, the other person—who has just talked about himself for an hour—will go out of his way to help you in return.

The Goal of Step Two

Step Two can take as little as one conversation and as much as several. By the end of all the talking, however, you want to make sure you know how to help them and they know how to help you.

Most people go about conversations absentmindedly. They don't put the puzzle pieces together, and that leaves everyone confused. Even if I want to help, I can't help if I don't know what they do or what they need. Referring legal clients to a doctor or dog-walking clients to a parakeet trainer would only frustrate everyone. Clear (non-pushy) goals make everyone's job easier. Offering the same from your side is courteous.

If the other person hasn't been clear how you can help them, ask. You'll be an outlier for asking and will earn goodwill, even if you're never able to connect them with a referral. Asking shows you care and are engaged.

STEP THREE: BUILDING TRUST AND STAYING TOP OF MIND

Once you've completed Step Two, if you can help the other person with something reasonable, you should. If they help you, accept the help gratefully. Every small interaction that builds trust will continue to build the relationship.

Sometimes, however, there's no way to help. Particularly in my field and many other fields that are "event-driven," the situation in question may not exist yet. For example, if you're a real estate agent, someone may not be in the market to buy or sell a house. In that case, don't worry about it, but stay in touch. If they have forgotten about you when they *are* in the market for a house, all your effort has been for naught.

Continue to follow up. Continue to have lunch and coffee and dinner in groups. When an opportunity arises to help, pursue it. Otherwise, wait. When the time is right, you'll already be top of mind. The person trusts you and understands what you do. They like you. When they need you, they will call. In the meantime, help them with a personal problem. Help them by sharing your (extended) network. Tell them where the best doughnuts are. It doesn't matter. Stay top of mind.

We'll spend more time in the next chapter unpacking exactly what it means to spend time in this third step, but for now, I'll reiterate: these things take time. Keep following up.

The results are worth it, and those results get better the longer you invest in building relationships.

STEP FOUR: STRATEGIC SERENDIPITY

We've talked about this last step before, so I won't spend too much time on it again. If you're a lawyer, or a real estate agent, or in my business, you'll need something to happen in your clients' lives before they need your services. Step Four happens when the event happens. If you've laid the groundwork, you'll be in the right place at the right time to get the call.

Hang out around the net. Be prepared, ready, and willing to jump when it's time to move. In the meantime, though, continue to follow up.

The business will arrive with strategic serendipity.

PATIENCE...TO A POINT

When I talk about this system, I emphasize patience. Relationships take time to build. Trust takes time to build. Results may not happen right away. However, you shouldn't be endlessly patient for no reason.

Stop being patient if, for whatever reason, the relationship stops feeling good. If it's not going anywhere, or you've stopped enjoying the person, stop investing in building the relationship.

For example, let's return to the real estate broker example. If the person you're trying to connect with is referring their friends to another broker, something broke down in the system. Either a) they don't know what you do; b) they have a deeper relationship with another broker; c) they don't think you're the right person; or a million other reasons, but you're not their broker now. The writing on the wall is clear. If the person is a friend and you don't care about the business side, then by all means, keep grabbing coffee. If this is a business relationship, however, it's time to look for more fertile fields.

Sometimes relationships will move out of their trust building stage quickly when it's time. We've established our *bona fides*, we know we want to work together, and there's that something else. It's platonic "love at first sight."

There are certain times in your life when you have that long-lost-friend feeling. You were introduced through a referral, you know what they do, and they know what you do. The stars align and you're ready to do business inside a week. Those are amazing moments, but they don't happen often. That said, I've found when you're open, they happen way more than I would have ever thought. For everyone else, you reach out with touchpoints, connect, and build trust for a long time.

For my business, I have to be top of mind at exactly the right moment. Those moments won't happen every day, and I know that. So I reach out, week by week, quarter by quarter, and wait.

I'm patient, and the universe takes care of me.

HACKING THE PROCESS

It's one thing to work steadily and patiently for results to happen; it's another to be patient for the sake of patience. If I can hack a process and spend half the time getting to the same end, you'd better believe I will.

Getting through all the stages of a business cycle can happen quickly. A personal introduction, like the one we gave Theresa, can earn a lot of trust out of the gate. We endorsed her, and that gave her social currency. I live off of and love referrals for this reason.

Other times, you can hack a business cycle by using credentials. If your business card says IBM or Goldman Sachs, people trust the name and trust you by association. You don't have to explain what you do or earn trust for as long a period.

I like to think of the business cycle in terms of the introduction, establishing likes, understanding what you do, really understanding what you do, following up, and the situation arises. You probably already understand what Goldman Sachs does. You may need to understand what a specific person at their company does, but you're primed to believe the person is highly educated, business-minded, reasonably trustworthy, and smart. That business card carries a lot of assumptions, allowing you to skip through the early stages of the business cycle more quickly. It's a very heavy card.

If you meet someone who's on his own or works for a small company you haven't heard of, the conversation is different. A new person will have many more questions. They'll be more cautious. My reality isn't a heavy card! I work in the context of a much smaller company, where people are cautious every step of the way. I've had to slog through all four phases of the cycle time and time again.

Goldman Sachs, or whatever other company we might use, provides a lot of legitimacy. It also takes a big cut of the dollars flowing through that business as a result. An independent contractor might get most of or all of the pie, but she'll have to hunt down the business and take it through the whole business cycle herself, from originating to executing to collecting the bills. There are upsides and downsides to both.

Becoming a rainmaker, even in a large company, means

building strategic relationships that will pay off for you. The difference is that rainmakers at large companies may not have to prove their *bona fides* for as long. All of the trust boxes have to be checked either way, but the large company's reputation may be checking them for you. At our company, we talk about hiring the front of the jersey versus the back of the jersey. My team members look to sell the front of the jersey, the company as a whole. If people are calling the back of the jersey, an individual person, we as a company need to keep working.

EVERYONE WANTS TO BE TOP OF MIND

Large organizations work at staying top of mind, too. They sponsor football games, golf events, and TED talks. They advertise. A potential client watches a golf match, sees a KPMG hat on someone, and thinks of their buddy at KPMG. If you work for KPMG, then, it's your job to differentiate yourself and be that guy's buddy.

If you're a five-person law firm, you won't be able to pay someone a million dollars to wear a hat with your firm's name on it at a nationally televised golf event. You will be able to pick up your phone and reach out with a touchpoint, however. Often that's enough.

Strategic relationship building lets you bring in money, and that gives you the power, control, and autonomy you need to build a work life that makes you happy. You can do the things you want to do, whether in the context of a large company, or a small company. I've worked in both places. Autonomy matters everywhere.

TRUST-BASED SALES

Not every business transaction requires a long trust-building process. If you need a screwdriver, you can drive down to the store and get a screwdriver. You don't have to have lunch with the screwdriver salesman first.

However, a lot of life involves relationships that feel higher stakes than just a screwdriver. You're hiring someone to help you find a house, or fix your business, or defend you in a lawsuit. You're hiring a coach to get you to the next level, or someone to find the right person to hire. The situation matters deeply to you—you'll need trust.

For me, transactional business feels like the speed dating world, impersonal and miserable. I don't really like it. Sometimes I'll just buy the screwdriver, if that's what I need, but I'd rather go down to the local hardware store and talk to the owner. She'll walk me through the choices, the bits, and which screwdriver will suit my project the best. If I pay a little more for a human experience, that's fine with me.

Even transactional businesses can be made better through relationships. My local hardware store has made money answering my questions better than its big-box competitor.

Any service that's high stakes or requires nuance and tailoring, however, absolutely requires relationship building. You're truly putting yourself in someone's hands. You're trusting them with your money, your career, your health, your social life, your business. It's not surprising that you want to do lunch with them first, to go through the human equivalent of dogs smelling each other at the dog park. You want to be sure they're okay.

Let's go back to the screwdriver example. There are probably hundreds of companies that sell screwdrivers. I'm guessing most sell similar products. When the salesman goes to the buyer at the hardware store, I'm guessing trust and relationships are critical in that transaction. The buyer wants to make sure he's getting good value and a good product, and the salesperson wants to make the sale over and over again. They both are invested in building a good relationship.

Humans are social creatures, just like dogs. We have to smell each other a bit before we're confident enough to do real business together. We want to go through the process and get comfortable being smelled.

A ONE-WORD EMAIL

Recently I sent my ubiquitous email to a buddy—you know the one. "Hey man, it's been too long. I feel bad we've fallen out of touch. Let's grab drinks or dinner. I hope you're well."

My buddy Hunter replied right away. "That's great, man, can you do next Thursday?" I told him that next Thursday was great, and then he ghosted me. He wasn't being mean, I think, just got busy and forgot. He's a very busy dude.

A day passed and a week passed, and I replied with a single word. "Dick."

He called me literally one minute later, laughing. He said it was the best email he'd gotten in three weeks, he was sorry for ghosting me, and we should set up a time for drinks. Then he invited me into a big business opportunity.

I've known Hunter for six years. We've spent a lot of time together and we've established our *bona fides*. He knows me and he likes me (or at least tolerates me if he's reading this!). What I love about relationship building, however, is that people tend to get more senior in their careers over time. Hunter was a good guy for me to know six years ago, but he's a great guy to know now. We've grown up in our careers together.

We started in a relatively transactional business relationship. He was a great lawyer at a great law firm. Over time, however, we've hit it off. We get tacos on Mondays. We've also found ourselves in a mutual admiration and benefit society—we bring each other tremendous business opportunities.

Hunter and I are dogs at the park sniffing, telling each other we're cool. We reach out to help each other, and we cement trust over and over. We also get to call each other dicks, and laugh. It's a fun time.

"WHAT HAVE YOU GOT?"

I would never go up to a businessperson I'd just met and ask for business. Relationships that begin with "what can you do for me?" feel wrong. They feel grabby and gross, like the little kids that always cut to the front of the line in elementary school. I used to tell my mom that I didn't like "firsty" people. I still don't. Demanding things doesn't feel human and warm, and that's not how I do business.

When a business relationship reaches a certain point, however, where trust and amicability have already been earned, suddenly the relationship becomes productive in a very particular way. I'll be sitting with a business friend eating bread or having a glass of wine, and part of the conversation naturally turns to "All right, man, how are we going to take over the world together? What have you got?" He tells me what business he has for me, and then he asks me, and I tell him.

Sometimes neither of us has business or opportunities for each other. That's fine. Oftentimes, however, we'll find ways to work together because we've had a lot of fun doing so in the past.

A productive business relationship absolutely starts with breaking bread, him helping me, me helping him, and shared time. Once you've gotten through all the steps, however, it eventually hits the point where we have enough transparency and intimacy. I spend an hour and a half hanging out and I enjoy every minute of that time. The real work of the meeting usually happens in five minutes near the end. I ask, "So what do you have you got? Anything we can work on? Here's what I'm working on."

With one friend, I might talk about the couple of deals we need help financing. "I can put you in touch with our guy who is handling that. Not sure if the deal is going to happen or not, but if it is, I think you'd be a good fit." With another, I might ask what work he has for me, and maybe something happens, maybe it doesn't.

At any given time, my firm is working for thirty to forty clients. I'm out talking to people, having donuts and coffee or dinner and drinks. We talk about our families. At a certain point, however, the gloves come off and we get very transactional. "You busy? You need stuff to do? How are you doing?" We connect people to other people and get deals done. One part of the network helps the other part.

Strategic relationship building happens with that end goal in mind.

A PERSONAL ASK

Recently my friend Ignatius asked me to go to the Dodgers game with him, and I agreed. I like the Dodgers.

The game was about three hours long, and it's baseball, so there was plenty of time to talk. We sat around eating popcorn and chitchatting. At one point he turned to me and told me that he's looking for a new job.

Great, I told him, and asked what he was looking to do. He told me he wanted to do the same thing in a different company. I ate my popcorn and thought a minute, and then I told him I'd introduce him to these other guys who might be looking. We talked back and forth for a minute about logistics, and then we went back to the game. The next day I made those phone calls for him.

Ignatius and I had been friends awhile—we'd built a certain level of intimacy. He was comfortable enough with me to tell me what he needed, and to trust me not to mess up his current job by telling his colleagues or making the wrong phone call. It took a few weeks, but Ignatius made an amazing career move. He'd landed a meeting at least partially from those phone calls I'd made for him—but he'd made it happen from that meeting.

Relationships—if you pour into them over time—can pay big dividends. You can rely on your network in situations like Ignatius's to help you out. You won't get that kind of result, however, if you don't put the work in at the beginning to level the relationship up.

THE BIG ASK

The business I run, at its most basic level, rents out people to do a service for clients. I call it a talent arbitrage. Think of a car rental agency. A car rental place that doesn't rent cars makes no money. Furthermore, the cars still require maintenance and the agency has to spend to stay in business, so every day they sit on the lot, money goes out the door. In the same way, if I don't have people working on things, having them sit around long enough gets financially dangerous.

I remember sitting at lunch one day with a good friend named Patrick. We had already finished our hamburgers, chitchatting while we waited for the bill to come. At that particular moment, my business was dramatically underutilized (which has happened maybe twice in ten years), and I knew I had the relationship standing with Patrick to speak up. So, I told him, "Hey, man, we need some work. You got anything?"

That conversation was two sentences. Like Ignatius did at the baseball game, I trusted Patrick to help me. Further, if he couldn't help me, I trusted him not to bust my image of a successful business guy at the one moment I was vulnerable. I was putting myself out there needing help and asking him to help me. As it happened, he showed up.

I fundamentally believe that most people want to help other people. We can be so afraid of asking for help because none of us wants to be that gross pushy sales guy. If you've built a strong relationship, however, it can withstand the ask. It almost requires the ask.

When you cross a certain threshold of relationship strength, there's a weird catalytic effect. The relationship goes from not transactional at all to being incredibly transactional. You become vulnerable and transparent, trusting the other person to show up for you.

When you have the trust in place, people show up.

MOVING RELATIONSHIPS FORWARD

No one gets to the kind of relationship where they can make big asks solely by sending short touchpoints. It takes a lot more than that! In the next chapter, we'll talk about all the details that go into maturing a relationship through the business cycle, from acorn to oak.

How do you connect with people in warm, authentic ways? How do you avoid common missteps that derail relationships before they're established? Most importantly, how do you dial in your energy and behavior so that you create productive, helpful relationships that feel good to everyone?

It's easier than you think.

Chapter Five

SOWING SEEDS

I went to a homecoming event at my college and ran into a guy we'll call Bob. We talked for five minutes at the event, and a week later he called me at work. To make it worse, he acted like we were closer than we were and immediately started pitching me to buy insurance from him. My annoyance was prodigious.

Over the next weeks, Bob kept calling. If I was ever going to buy insurance from Bob, I certainly wasn't at that point, but he kept calling even more. I would see his name on the Caller ID and literally wince. Please don't be Bob.

If Bob had been more educated on this technique, he'd have taken a softer approach. He'd have reached out once and told me how great it was to see my family. Then he would have said something like, "I remember we didn't spend that much time together in college, but I always wanted to. If you're ever in Orange County or vice versa, I'd love to catch up. It sounds like you're doing great, and I would love to reconnect after all of this time. Hope you're well."

If Bob and I had then hit it off, and he'd followed up, we might have built the kind of relationship where I would have bought insurance, and likely referred several friends. Even though we weren't close in college, it's perfectly possible that common bond from all those years ago could be the start of business relationship or even a friendship. Unfortunately, he overplayed his hand and folded the relationship before it ever began.

I still think of Bob and wince.

WHO TO APPROACH

How do you build your career by networking? I often tell people to start with people you knew and have fallen out of touch with, as I've mentioned several times in this book. You can also find new people at networking events, yoga class, at the school drop-off line, or wherever else you go in your life.

If you're in professional services, however, also be sure to reach out to the clients you're working on or have worked for in the past. An accountant, for example, might do a job with a controller at ABC Manufacturing Company. You can't help but get to know somebody reasonably well when you're working side by side through an intense project. There's a camaraderie developed through mutual experience.

Some period of time after the day-to-day interaction is over, the accountant might email the controller saying, "Hey, I was wondering how everything is going over there. I remember the forecast were saying that big things were coming, so I was wondering how it all ended up. Would love to catch up with you." Relate to the person on something they care about, but the specifics of whether the forecast was up 2 percent or 4 percent don't matter. The fact that you remember working on that forecast with them will make a connection. The connection starts a relationship, which might grow naturally into coffee or drinks.

It's useful to build connections with people within your industry ecosystem, but it's also worthwhile to connect with people on the fringes. Having advocates in complimentary, or completely different, industries can be immensely helpful. Being the only consultant somebody knows in my field has served me well over the years. They don't know much about my competitors, so I can frame my industry for them without the baggage of other experiences.

That's not to say that people infinitely far away from your industry are as helpful. You may not want to befriend your dog walker, unless you genuinely like him and want to be friends with him for his own sake. (Friendship is always a great outcome with great people, regardless of industry.)

Building a network deliberately does mean spending your time to connect dots with people who can help you. Look at other pockets within your organization. Network with other people at your firm, at industry events, professional events, and anyone in a business environment.

In the legal world, for example, you'll network at industry conferences, training classes, with competitors, clients, and anyone with whom you don't have a conflict. Network with people trying to sell things to you. There will always be people trying to sell things to you, and often they have very large networks to share in return.

Virtually anyone you meet in a professional environment is worth chitchatting with. Chat and see where it goes. You're there anyway, so why not use that time strategically?

YOUR CLIENTS CAN HELP GROW YOUR CAREER

Believe it or not, your clients can help you grow your career, particularly if they're on the fringes of your industry.

Let's return to the accounting example from above. Once you—as an accountant—have a rapport with the person at ABC Manufacturing Company, you might eventually be vulnerable and talk about your current job. You'll talk about how you like the company, but you've been there a long time and are looking forward to being promoted.

If the person is tuned in and you have a relationship, they might echo that the company you're working for is great. Or perhaps they'll mention their connection to another accounting firm that might have a better job for you. The conversation comes once the relationship is established.

The more people you talk to in such low-key, non-pressuring ways, the more likely it is that you'll find someone who helps. Believe me. People love to help. If they can help you, they can feel good about themselves, and they will have built their own networks. We all know that people tend to feel loyalty to the person who helps them.

That said, mind your words: be careful not to bad-mouth your boss or present company. You want to stay on good terms, yes. More importantly, you want to make the conversation about you and your ambitions, not about the firm you're at. People understand ambition, and they'll listen if you're authentic.

After you start your new job, in a year or so, follow up with your current boss and coworkers with touchpoints. If you stay on good terms, they, too, can grow your network.

WHAT MAKES A REAL CONNECTION?

As you build strategic relationships, keep in mind that not every contact will be either a buddy or a friend, and filing a name away in your contacts isn't enough. Relationships don't exist in theory or on paper. People you knew ten years ago aren't your network if you never talk to them again. Relationships are made of real human connections.

For these to be real relationships, you have to actually do what you do in relationships: relate. Putting a person in your contact list, your LinkedIn network, or filed away in a stack of business cards isn't enough. You must stay in touch. The number of friends, followers, or likes you have doesn't matter. What matters is picking up the phone, text, or email and having people at the other end of the line remember you and think fondly of you.

Connections don't have to be profound or personal. Even a surface touchpoint now and again makes you more memorable and more relatable than the dozens of other people doing what you do. LeBron might have two hundred LinkedIn friends that work for the same financial advisory firm, but he remembers Marla, because she listened well when he talked to her. That relationship may be based on one conversation and a touchpoint now and then, but it's a real connection.

Relationships aren't made on broadcast. They're crafted one at a time, carefully, by hand.

Don't Be Pushy

I once had a salesman track down my personal cell phone number after I'd talked with him at an event. He sent me a text message out of nowhere. If he'd been calling me, it would have been a cold call. Given that he was texting me, it felt offensive and intrusive.

I don't think I'm alone in this, but I don't like to get calls from people who aren't in my phone. The one exception is people who were such good friends they're besties from another era. Those people I'll be glad to hear from in ten years—but everyone else? No.

The salesman ruined whatever chance he might have had with me (already slim) by choosing the wrong medium. The right approach would probably have been email, or a LinkedIn message, usually with some reference as to what detective work they went through to get my contact information. Likely, without a connection from an event or a previous relationship, I would still have deleted the message, but I wouldn't have been annoyed about it.

If you're on the fence between two communication methods, choose the less personal of the two. It's always better to have someone pull you in with more warmth rather than have them annoyed because you've over-presumed.

The Intimacy Scale

Relationships tend to fall somewhere on a scale between casualness and depth, with the thing that's changing being called, for lack of a better term, intimacy. I tend to under-presume intimacy rather than over-presume.

What does that mean in practice? If I haven't talked to someone in a few years, I assume they haven't been thinking of me. I start at a step below wherever we last left the relationship. So if we were slight friends, I might assume he or she doesn't even remember me. "I don't know if you even remember me, but we were in the same English class together [or used to work in the same cubicles that time]. I remember this one time we did this thing and I remember enjoying the conversations. I'd love to catch up sometime."

Starting at a relatively casual level of intimacy doesn't presume. You're sharing a memory about them rather than asking anything of them. It's completely inoffensive and incontrovertible. If you had said you remembered that you were best friends, that would be different—you'd be presuming a level of comfort and intimacy that's probably not there. I find it bothersome when someone claims to be my close friend when they're not. It feels fake.

I'd rather under-presume and have someone correct me than over-presume and do as that salesman did to crash the relationship. Saying, "hey there, old buddy, old pal," when we weren't buddies or pals feels pushy. Too pushy, and people shut you out for good.

On the other hand, if I start more distant and people felt warmth for me, they'll often be willing to bring me in closer. Worst case, I gauge the relationship correctly, and we'll be able to connect at the right level. When you under-presume, you never feel pushy, and you're never taken as pushy. The sweet "of course I remember you" is a gateway to a new, warm relationship.

HAVING THE RIGHT ENERGY

I had breakfast with a guy yesterday who had a business similar to a buddy's. I connected them, saying, "you guys probably know similar people, so you should talk." Perhaps there will be a business deal that happens as a result of that introduction. Perhaps there won't. Either way I'll have helped facilitate the meeting, and both will think well of me.

Creating touchpoints serves several masters. Communities and networks have inherent value. Helping people has inherent value. At the most transactional level, however, the practice of touchpoints also builds mutually beneficial business relationships. You can sell more of your goods and services and that other person can sell more as well.

I'm an unabashed business guy. I spend a lot of time building my business, my brand, and my network. From a certain point of view, then, building strategic relationships might seem like I'm using people. I absolutely do not see it that way. I'm taking opportunities to uplift people and allow them to uplift me. I'm getting opportunities to help.

People have inherent value. Just as importantly, building bridges between people is enjoyable. Every pleasant conversation, particularly with someone you wouldn't otherwise connect with, is a win. Going into relationships for what you can get out of them feels gross. Taking an attitude of helpfulness feels right.

I believe we get back the kind of energy we put out into the universe. Which would you rather get back, help and value or people looking to use you? Stick to creating good energy, and you won't receive as many bad vibes in return.

COMMON INTERESTS

Pay attention to the other person—you're looking to dial in what kind of person they are and what they like to do. What is their lifestyle like? Who are they as a person? What are they interested in, and what times do they actually have available?

If I'm talking to a forty-eight-year-old guy with kids, sometimes it's easy to meet him for a drink after work, but I've found it's often more common for guys in this category to be home at five o'clock for family time every night. If that's the case, I'll ask for a breakfast meeting or coffee or something similar. If he talks about dinner with his kids, I won't ask for a time after work unless he suggests it first.

In a different situation, perhaps with a gal who's always talking about the cool restaurants she and her husband have been to, I notice that she's an out and about person. In that case, I'd suggest getting a group of work friends together for dinner at the new Bangladeshi fusion place in town. She likes food, and it makes sense to connect over food in a group.

Focus on the interests that you and the other person have in common. If you like art, you'll talk about art, and it will feel natural to mention the new art exhibit down the street and suggest a trip. If you're the kind of person who watches hockey or *Game of Thrones,* talk about those events. The people who'll connect with you will be on board.

Keep an eye on meeting someone where they are, however. Talk about their interests, specifically, whenever it feels natural to do so. People like talking about themselves and their interests. But keep it natural.

(By natural, I mean be a human being. Sales training emphasizes that people like hearing their names said frequently, but I always feel like someone is overselling if they say my name too much. "Larry, I need to talk about what Larry wants, because if Larry gets what he wants, I'm happy." Yuck. Lay off the gimmicks. Be authentically human first, and the rest will come.)

Anything you like and want to talk about can be fodder for an interesting conversation and a moment of connection. You have to be vulnerable enough to put yourself out there, however. You have to be willing to show who you are, even in just a very small way.

ON VULNERABILITY

People get afraid of showing any vulnerability in a work context. However, no one likes a robot. If you go to work, play golf, and go home, people will struggle to connect with you. Building relationships means showing some vulnerability, sharing your life and your likes.

Too much vulnerability, however, is also a problem. Especially with the more peripheral relationships in your life, too much vulnerability becomes intense and uncomfortable. Telling someone you're having trouble with your wife or your dad is dying can overstress a casual relationship to the point of breaking.

So how do you know where the line is?

For most relationships I tend to stick to the topics I'd discuss with a barber or nail person. I'll talk about my kids, or the improv class I'm thinking about, or a movie I've seen. At this level of conversation, if something I said shows up on the front page of the newspaper, it's fine. In fact, I'd find it funny.

I also tend to share details that can fit within my overall brand. Someone looking at my LinkedIn page will see I'm a business guy who works for a consulting firm. Finding out that the business guy who works for the consulting firm also loves spy novels and self-help and cooking changes nothing. None of that is remotely controversial, and if anything, it makes me look more human.

I tend to save true emotional vulnerability for people who are close friends. Talking about hopes, dreams, and fears is a different level of connection, and there are relationships for which that's appropriate and helpful. Sometimes sharing those things can become the path to friendship. Friendship is incredibly worthwhile, and I value my friends greatly.

However, the point of this system is to enjoy every relationship for what it is, even if it's a light and cursory one where you mostly talk about cats. I don't have to make a relationship be more than it is. I can enjoy the cats and keep it light. And by the way, maybe that bond over cats helps us in business.

BE CAREFUL WITH ESCALATION

If you do coffee with someone, do coffee again. If you texted, text again. Don't jump from coffee to dinner with spouses— you'll overstep the relationship and make people shut down.

"That was fun, let's do it again" should be your rallying cry. If you're meeting someone for a playdate for the kids at the park, text to suggest you meet at the park again. Doing the same thing in the same place is noncontroversial. It's light, and easy to agree with.

You become lunch buddies with someone, and that's what you do. If you're a pen pal, enjoy being a pen pal. Sometimes relationships will advance from there naturally, and sometimes they won't. If you develop from acquaintance to buddy to friendship to close friendship over time, great. Otherwise, enjoy the relationship for what it is.

If you've met your long-lost sister or brother from another mother and the feeling is clearly returned, escalate. If you meet someone and the conversation is stilted and awkward, don't follow up. For everyone else in the middle, however, go slow and steady. Repeat the same coffee, lunch, or sandwich run until it either develops on its own or stays steady as a nice, pleasant part of your life. You can always use another sandwich buddy at work, after all.

Pay Attention to Your Feelings

I've found over the years that my body will tell me when I've overstepped in a relationship. I get a physical sensation in my gut that's unpleasant. I literally feel bad.

Last week I was introduced to a guy named Peter through a law firm friend of mine. Peter is a sharp person that does financial advisory work for guys like me. He and I met up for coffee with a mutual law firm friend, but the conversation went awry. The friend ended up talking about something going on with her for the entire time.

Peter, who appears to be as tuned in to the same wavelength on relationships as I am, emailed me the next day. "Hey, man, nice meeting you. We only got a second to talk, but I've heard a lot of nice things about you. That story with Beatrice was pretty crazy. If you're up for it, let's grab some time on the phone over the next week so we can figure out how we can help each other." That interaction was innocuous and pleasant.

If, however, Peter had shifted to introducing me to his underwriting team, my gut would churn with that unpleasant feeling. Wait, I thought we were friends, what happened?

We'll talk about this more in the next chapter, but there's a right way to build a business relationship. I want to get to know someone, like them, and trust them a little bit before

I ever hear what they're selling. If someone skips steps, my gut objects.

When I accidentally skip a step (though I haven't done it in a while), I get the same physical objection from the other end. Listen to your feelings and use them as a guide to avoid moving too fast.

When you overstep, apologize if you can, and deescalate. Sometimes, however, you just have to move on. The fact is, if you're doing this right, you're going to meet a lot of people! Some won't want to connect for whatever reason. Live, let live, and move on to the next connection.

The Rank Order of Meetings

Strategic connection building is a numbers game. You'll want to make as many meaningful contacts as you can, but you won't be able to have dinner with everyone. (There are only so many dinners in a week!) Therefore, you'll want to deliberately keep people at a lower level of intimacy—which means carefully avoiding escalation. In addition, most people will be more comfortable if you don't come on too strong, too fast. Keeping the relationship light benefits everyone.

There are certain relationships you maintain that are more obviously business. Spending time and effort to maintain those makes sense. However, I also spend time building relationships that don't have an obvious connection. Black swan events happen in everyone's life now and again. That's why I invest in many light relationships. Will I choose an established, productive business relationship over a light connection in terms of the priority I give it? Most of the time yes. However, I do build those lighter relationships on purpose even so.

So how do you keep relationships light and avoid escalation? It's helpful to understand where different meetings stack up in terms of rank order so that you can avoid going up the chain unintentionally.

Some get-togethers are "weightier" than others. In general, unless you have a reason to jump the line, you'll want to stay as light as possible and on the same level. You want to be warm and friendly but non-pressuring. You want to feel easy to be around. Staying light is part of how you create that feeling.

At the bottom of the rank order, the easiest and least weighty meeting, is coffee. It's almost easier to get someone out for coffee than even to a meeting at their office. Everyone likes coffee, and it doesn't feel like a big commitment.

A meeting at the office is the next easiest to set up; it's a fact of life that you will need an actual business agenda (even if light) to justify attention on a Thursday at 2:00 pm, but it's easy and feels not at all pressuring. Next heaviest is lunch and then drinks.

At the "heaviest" end of the scale is dinner, or even more so, dinner with the spouses. That one you should only set up when you've known someone for a long time, or you both clearly feel a strong connection.

Many people forget about the group option, which sits between lunch and dinner. I like the dynamic that comes from groups, personally, so I often say something like, "put me in touch with a group of your guys, I'll put you in touch with a group of mine, and we'll set up a group to take over the world." Drinks or dinner with four or five people tends to be a lot less awkward, with fewer weird silences, than a one-on-one event, and there's no possibility of an accidental dating vibe.

I like groups for another reason as well. Groups give you a wider reach for the same time commitment. In the spirit of service, also, groups provide amazing opportunities to connect people within your network. Maybe I'm not interesting to a person, but the four or five people I'll bring with me will be. Perhaps two of them will hit it off and become tennis buddies or business partners.

Again, be careful with escalation. Escalate slowly, or not at all; you'll want to keep it easy and light indefinitely. So, in a situation where I feel good, I'll say something like, "I thought this was just going to be a regular business lunch, but I really enjoyed this. Let's do it again soon." Usually if the vibe is warm, most people will gladly do another coffee or a lunch. I don't escalate. I'm not in a rush, and not every acquaintance is meant to be a buddy, and not every buddy a friend. At its basic level, coffee is thirty minutes and a small bill in your pocket. Dinner is a bigger investment of both time and treasure. Enjoy people for who they are, where they are, and stay as light as makes sense.

AN INTENTION OF MOVING FORWARD

I find that I'm more able to relax and enjoy the process when I can be intentional. When I first meet someone, I focus on deciding whether this is a person I'd like to spend more time with. If I do want to stay in touch, how do I want to stay in touch? How often, and using what medium?

Once I'm in touch with someone, in the early stages I do something I call trying to preserve optionality. I try to hold space to engage in a conversation. The early stages can often be a little uncertain. What does this person do? What role will he or she play in my life? Even in situations where it's obvious the person is a work contact, it can take a little while for the relationship to develop. I wait to see where it goes.

When you have someone you've established a relationship with, on the other hand, eventually you'll reach a point where you will become transactional. Are you showing up to have fun and be social? Set that intention. Are you wanting to gain business or set up a deal? Be more explicit about that intention. Once you've set up the trust and essential underpinnings of a working friendship, for example, be ready to ask. Just be sure you're asking how you can help as well, just as frequently.

Always, always continue to go in with an attitude of helpfulness. People can feel that attitude.

AVOIDING THE CREEPY FACTOR

I've often been asked how the "non-platonic" relationship factor plays into strategic relationship building. Basically, how do I navigate relationships without coming across as creepy?

I'm careful to be mindful during interactions of that potential for creepiness and cut it off at the pass. I discuss my wife and daughter early (sometimes awkwardly early) and proudly wear a wedding ring. I put out a strong signal that I'm not here for developing romantic or sexual relationships, so I don't come across as creepy.

That being said, even before I was a family man, it wasn't as hard as people make it sound to avoid the sexual vibe. When you're not pushy and not asking for a date, when you keep the interaction light and fun, focusing on the warm interaction and nothing else, the dynamic tends to take care of itself. People tend to pick up on whatever energy you are sending out.

Because people are people, and things happen, I wanted to make the point. If this is the reason that you're not getting out there a meeting new people, it's super easy to nip this one in the bud. Put out a businesslike, warm, friendly energy, and make connections widely.

PRIORITIES

Let's say you've been building relationships strategically for a while now. The good and bad part about this system is that it tends to take on a life of its own. It's like a snowball rolling down a mountain. When you reach out to ten to thirty people per week, your calendar will fill up with fun things and interesting people.

Eventually, you'll have so many abundant relationships that you'll need to prioritize. Lunch happens only once per day (unless you're a hobbit). In practice, no matter how much you like everyone on your list, you'll be limited as to the number of people you can see in person in a given time frame. That's fine. Not every connection will be a friend, or even a buddy.

The hardest part about this system is how to manage your life when you've reached the place of abundance. You only have so much energy and time. So how do you decide? I like to tune in to how I'm feeling about the relationship in question. Certain people give me more excitement. It's important to note that those relationships aren't necessarily business ones. Every time my friend Ari calls me, I take the call, because I enjoy those conversations. Ari isn't a business connection, he's a pure friend. We connect in a way that gives me joy.

Some relationships, on the other hand, end up feeling forced. I'm stalling on things to say, and we never make it from the interactions at the conferences to actually getting coffee. When relationships stall out, I let them. It doesn't mean I can't continue to see someone at events; it means that I don't push the relationship to be more than it is.

With communication methods, meetings, and everything else, I find relationships tend to find their level. Some friends I only text, some people I only email, and some buddies I connect with over every communication method. I've even had people I only see over lunch, our assistants setting everything up without our involvement.

Some people are people you only see every so often, conference buddies or that guy you get a beer with after work every now and then. Others light you up, and those you'll make a point of connecting with. You'll reply to texts promptly. You'll reach out to them more often. Let your feelings be your guide. If you use a scheduling system, schedule people who excite you—or can help you—every month or two. Schedule people who excite you less or who can help you less perhaps only every three or six months.

I tend to focus on one part of life at a given time, and often I'll seek out people who can help me with that project or area. Sometimes work is giving me happiness, so I chase that harder. Other times, I want to connect with good friends or talk with someone who has a different point of view on the world, so I'll seek out those people. As a result, the people I connect with tend to ebb and flow over time. That's fine, too.

I keep a very full plate of relationships. If I'm feeling more blah, I'll get more deliberate about seeking people out who give me energy. Who's somebody that I look up to, where every time I sit with them, I have a good laugh?

Building touchpoints should be a pleasant experience for everyone. I let relationships be what they are, and don't try to push them any deeper than they naturally want to go.

Rico, a guy who used to be an enemy and is now a good friend, is inspiring to me. He's advised me on some big business projects and has become almost rabbinical to me. I don't over-ask, but when I need a shot in the arm on the business side, sometimes I'll call Rico. When I need a different kind of energy, I call a different kind of person.

What do you need in your life right now? Who can you reach out to who might help with that? Go with what feels important in your life at the moment, and the conversations that result will feel natural.

DELIBERATE PRIORITIES

I'm a very goal-driven guy. As such, I'm not just seeking out people to talk football with. I make friends, and I have friends, but my focus in relationship building usually falls in line with my other ambitious goals.

Often the relationships I'm building are, in fact, ones designed to help me in business. Other times, I'm pursuing ambitious goals on the charitable side. My overall strategic rubric of life has room for goals in business and community and family. When it's time to connect more with the family, I'll seek out people who might be able to help me go deeper in that arena.

The point is that I don't just take whatever relationships show up and call that good enough. I choose to pursue relationships that fall in line with the things that are most important to me within my larger life goals. What are your goals? Who can you talk to who might be able to help you make progress on them?

Use this system with your entire life. Not only will it make you happier, but you will connect more with other people. We all have lives outside of work. Tapping into those lives feels authentic and good. Ending up too divorced into the business side only ends up feeling forced and robotic. It turns people off. We're all whole people. You'll be more authentic when you can approach people as whole humans, with a deep appreciation for who they are at that moment. This means being open to tennis buddies as well as work buddies, but also being willing to discuss cats or gardening or anything else. Be open to all connections. No one is "just" a stockbroker.

I've found that when I'm happier at work, I'm happier in my personal life—and vice versa. At one point, I was very interested in improv classes. You would not believe the fun conversations I was able to have with businesspeople around improv classes. It worked because it was truly what was going on in my life at the time. Having a life outside of business matters.

PEOPLE HELP YOU

Life isn't meant to be lived alone. Follow up and talk about your life. Help others. Do the work, and trust that good things will happen.

My entire philosophy is that people help your life be better, whether in small ways or large ones. You can't and won't know which relationship will do what for you, nor should you look at it as purely transactional. Rather, put yourself in the hands of the people in your life so that they (as a group) can help you advance your goals. Help them in return, help them first, and trust that your needs will also be taken care of.

If you're deliberate about building relationships, your life will grow better and faster than it would otherwise. You'll be able to leverage those great people in your world that can and want to help you.

For many of us, asking for help isn't easy. It's often even harder to accept help. Allow help to come your way—help in the form of referrals, or even a great conversation in which you feel heard. Don't turn people away or shut down help out of your own insecurities. If you won't accept help, why reach out to build relationships in the first place?

Relax, and trust that people are helping for good reasons. Take the help when people offer it, knowing that you yourself will help others in return and everyone will be uplifted for the exchange.

Reciprocity is important, but notice how I phrased the sentence. You won't always return help to the exact same person who offered you help in the first place. Many times, those who you help won't be able to help you immediately in return. However, help can't be a one-way street. You can't drive around the world one way, or let others drive you. You get back from the universe the energy you put in.

Whether you want to call it karma or the law of attraction, every time you put good things out there, they do make their way back to you. On page three of my bullet journal I have a list of each and every cosmic return I've seen. I call it the signs of an abundant universe, and I look at them often.

When you choose the people you want in your life, whether those relationships are deep or shallow, you choose the people who can help your life get better. You aren't using them. You should be helping them with their lives as well.

Chapter Six

OFFERING AND ASKING FOR HELP

Like everyone else, I met Calvin through lunch with a mutual friend. When Calvin followed up a couple of weeks later, he reminded me he'd met me through Kyle and connected with me in a warm, unassuming way. We eventually sat down for lunch, and he gave me a copy of the book he'd written about his family, in a way that was both vulnerable and charming.

He hosts regular curated dinners to introduce people, so I went to one. He's connected me with fascinating and inspiring people who happen to be in town. He introduced me to his business coach. At one point, he downloaded all of his LinkedIn contacts and said, if there's anyone on this list you'd like to meet, let me know and I'll introduce you. He was so generous with his network that at first it was a little off-putting. That kind of generosity felt so odd, however, that I had to see it again. He was memorable.

It took me a year and a half to find out what he did for a living. Right about the time I discovered that Calvin sold insurance, I was ready to buy.

Four years later, Calvin has sold me nearly all my insurance. And I've indirectly introduced Calvin to maybe thirty-five other people, many of whom also eventually bought insurance from him. His generosity turned into a very productive relationship for him, but in a context that feels warm and nice for both of us. I consider him a friend.

STANDING OUT IN A COMMODITY MARKET

The insurance industry, like many industries, is very much a commodity market. Everyone literally sells the same product. Furthermore, Calvin is hardly unique—there are seven million people who sell insurance in the United States. By the numbers, Calvin should be in trouble.

However, Calvin has found a way to transcend the other millions of insurance guys out there. He comes across as authentic, interesting, and helpful—because he is—and before long people buy.

No one (maybe not even I) takes relationship building as far as Calvin does. He has systems to keep track of it all, with files full of notes on people. The effort he puts in stands well beyond what most of us can afford to spend in terms of time. However, Calvin succeeds professionally based entirely on his network, and the help he provides to people without expecting anything in return.

Before long, you feel so good about Calvin, you start to ask him about his insurance.

THE RIGHT OFFER

A few years back I met a guy named Kevin in the wealth management business. I was a candidate for someone who might be able to use his services, but he didn't try to sell me. Instead, he said, "I'd love to figure out ways where I can introduce you to people who might be able to help you build your business."

What's notable about Kevin's offer was not just the offer, though that was generous in its own right. What's notable is how much he had paid attention. At that moment I wasn't looking to expand my charity work, or to connect more with my family. I wasn't looking to get my child into preschool or thinking about summer camp. I was full-bore focused on expanding my company.

Kevin listened, helped, and impressed me.

HOW CAN YOU HELP?

Be like Kevin. Pay attention to the people around you and their current needs. What is she interested in right now? What is keeping him up at night? Helping someone build her business is great—if that's where they are. Otherwise, help with summer camp, or finding the best movie to see, or the best place to stay in New York.

Spend the time to truly *listen* to people, and to meet them where they are. I know nothing about how to solve someone's engineering problem. However, I can listen, or I can recommend my favorite babysitter to help her find a little extra time to solve the problem, or perhaps I can introduce her to another engineer who might be able to help. In none of those cases was I offering to introduce her to someone to build her business. That wasn't what she needed at that moment.

How much time should you spend on someone else's problem? As with most questions in life, the answer is "it depends." If it's a person you really care about, or a possibly important person in your life, or someone who could really help you, spend more time. If the person isn't a priority, or you just don't have the space right now, spend less time. We all must prioritize the twenty-four hours we get in a day, and not every connection will be the highest priority in your life at that time.

However, some connections are higher priority and worth

the effort. I once spent an entire day early in my career figuring out the best places to stay in New York on short notice for a client. The client I helped eventually brought me a lot of business. I'd do it again, though these days I'm often able to help with less effort in other ways. Helping is how I do business.

THE LADDER OF HELP

I like to think of ability to help in terms of a ladder. You might be further up or further down the rungs of that ladder at this point in your career. As you move up in your career, you move up the ladder.

Sometimes you have an opportunity, like I did, to spend time helping someone further up the ladder with a problem, like I helped the client with his trip to New York. Later in your career, you might have an opportunity like the ones I have now, to help people succeed with a few well-placed phone calls.

Say we have Jennifer, who's a hiring manager at a large company, and Andy, a person who wants to work for that large company. Jennifer needs to find good people for the role, and Andy wants to be the person hired. If Jennifer is asking her network where a good place to go for her anniversary dinner is, if the question comes to him, Andy should spend hours if necessary doing all the research to find the best answer.

Giving her a good answer differentiates him from all the other candidates.

On the other hand, if Andy asks Jennifer the same question at an industry mixer, Jennifer has a long list of other priorities. She shouldn't spend the time to do that research. But if Jennifer knows a hiring manager at a different company who might be looking for Andy, she should make that phone call.

Put another way, you don't ask Richard Branson where to go to dinner in New York. Introducing me to someone at the Virgin Group, in contrast, would be easy for him to do and far more helpful to me.

As you go further up the ladder, meaning the corporate ladder, the experience ladder, and so forth, you naturally collect resources. Your knowledge gets broader. You know more people after twenty years in a community than you do after two. As such, the farther along you travel in life, the easier it becomes to reach into your bag, so to speak, and grab something that will help someone. In the beginning, you might have to do research and create a way to help out of whole cloth. Later, you'll carry around resources to help people, and it becomes a matter of which resources to use.

Richard Branson probably isn't going to help me at this moment. Even if he wanted to, he has other priorities, and I don't fault him for choosing them. However, if I was in a position to help Richard Branson get his granddaughter into preschool, and that's something he was actively looking for, I'd do whatever it took to make that happen.

Helping is the right thing to do, and like Calvin, I try to be as generous as I can be to a wide range of people. That said, sometimes I choose to help certain people disproportionately for whatever reason. Sometimes it's someone I care about, sometimes it's someone who can help me more in return, and sometimes the stars align that day and I'm able to do it. Helping people is an investment, sometimes a big one, but it's how I do business. I'd recommend you do the same.

MORE CHARLIE, LESS VERUCA

I met Karlos at another endless cocktail party. (You can see why I go to those things despite the terrible food.) We chitchatted, and it turned out we had mutual friends, and our conversation went from there. At one point, he told me he wasn't happy with his job anymore, and I introduced him to potential employers. Once he landed, we talked about how we could do a joint venture together.

After six or seven years, Karlos and I have worked on five different major projects together. I didn't go into our first lunch saying, "What can you do for me?" The relationship grew over time—to our mutual financial benefit, I might add.

SERVANT LEADERSHIP

While we're on the subject of having the right attitude and being helpful, I'll mention another key part of my business philosophy. Find ways to help your team help you. Lean into servant leadership.

In the old generation, there was 1950s authoritarian command and control. In the millennial world, the power dynamic has shifted radically toward the employee. This is largely a good thing—empowered people bring innate creativity and value to work in ways they don't when they feel like cogs in a wheel. However, supporting empowered employees takes extra work from leadership, work you have to plan for.

As I'm writing this book, I'm looking at a whiteboard covered with cultural initiatives. We work hard to make our company a better place to work for our people. I'd rather spend the time figuring out how to help my employees succeed through servant leadership than setting up better mousetraps to command and control them. Empowered people bring more to the table. Helping them do their jobs effectively is the least I can do.

No company exists without the group of people working within it. The brick and mortar don't matter. How well the people within the company work together, in a professional services context, is literally the difference between the business living and dying. Servant leadership strengthens the company and improves the work. It systemically improves peoples' ability to work better together, and it's the right thing to do.

I had a conversation with my business partner yesterday. We were complaining that we couldn't track down a particular person, because we keep flexible hours and a liberal work from home policy. My business partner asked me, "How do the big firms in New York do it?" He looked at me, I looked at him, and then we laughed. The big firms in New York don't do it. They keep people chained to their desks nine to five (or five to nine).

If people hate working someplace and leave after two years, all the knowledge they've accumulated walks out the door with them. I enjoy helping people. I build relationships out in the world. It feels only right, then, to empower and help people in the context of work at my company. The same philosophical system works for both. I also believe I get more out of my people as a result.

I believe in servant leadership. If you help other people, they want to follow you. Telling someone to do something by saying, "I'll pay you more," isn't leadership. It's paying them money to do a thing. If you can get people to show up for you and believe in you, that's leadership.

By going out into the community and making relationships with people you help, you're practicing leadership. Strategic relationship building will help you bring in more business opportunities and promotions and find career opportunities, friends, lovers, what have you. It builds a network of people who support you and follow you. When you do it correctly, by its very nature, building relationships makes you a leader.

If I'd been Veruca Salt from *Charlie and the Chocolate Factory*, if I'd gone into that relationship with a gimme-gimme attitude, it would have been gross. Karlos and I would never have worked together. By being humble and other-focused like Charlie Bucket, however, I was able to make a connection that's improved my life.

By looking to help and not to take, I was able to build another relationship that has literally enriched me. Look to make connections in your own life with a similar attitude.

THE ASK

Remember Jack, who networked his way into a meeting with the VP of a large national bank? Jack blew his meeting by spending all of it on pleasantries. We all like connecting over jazz and college stories, but at 2:00 pm on a Tuesday we also expect a business agenda.

Part of strategic relationship building is knowing when and how to ask. If you hear nothing else in this section, hear this: the relationship has to be strong enough to support the ask. (I'll talk more about how to build and strengthen a relationship in the next chapter.) A stronger relationship can support a stronger ask. Sometimes, however, a cursory relationship can also support a cursory ask.

In the situation with Jack and the VP, the senior guy took

the meeting at his office. He liked Jack. He was expecting a small ask. The right way to approach that situation, once you're there, is something like the following. "I don't want to take up too much of your time. I work with this firm here. My firm works with firms like yours all the time. I'd love to set up a time with my CEO and you to just talk over things a little bit. I think it'd be a really productive conversation."

By asking in a quick, non-pressuring way, you're framing the situation as not just being friends for the sake of being friends. In the context of a meeting at 2:00 pm on a Tuesday, that ask will actually make a VP relax. Jack was very good at getting in the room by being interesting and charming, but by failing to ask, he made the other party question why he was there. It felt uncomfortable.

You should always establish the rapport first. Then, tailor your ask to the level of rapport. If I'm in a situation with a meeting that's unexpectedly turned chilly, I've been known to ask and get out. "I know you're really busy. The only reason I'm here is to have a quick five-minute conversation and put a face on a name. We're a management consulting firm and we'd love to do more work with the bank. If there's someone on your team you think we should work with, great. I appreciate your taking the time to meet me."

In a situation where I'm there because I have a warm buddy or friend relationship with someone, I'll make my ask more personal. "Thanks for meeting me. It was great to see you at that event. How's your wife? Listen, I'm really trying to do well in my company. I'd love to set up an introduction between you and my CEO just to figure out if there are ways we all can work together. It would really make me look good." By framing the request more personally, you're putting yourself out there on the friendship side. That's a perfectly reasonable thing to do if the relationship is there.

Standard sales systems can feel icky to people. Building relationships, on the other hand, should feel warm and natural. It feels fine to mention to someone you're connecting with that, "This is the company I work for. I'm generally looking to work with these kinds of people. If anything comes up, let me know." There's no pushiness there.

Know what your goal is for a conversation before you show up. In most cases, if the relationship is there, go ahead and talk about why you're there. Don't be afraid of small asks. But also don't be afraid to ask how you can help.

DIALING IN THE ASK

You'll get better at matching the level of asks to the level of relationship over time. If you under-ask, the relationships will end up feeling unproductive and unmoored. If you over-ask, people will say no, and sometimes walk away. You'll have to develop a feel for how and when to ask through experience.

I generally tend to focus first on how I can be helpful and ask later.

Don't belabor the ask. You don't take something awkward and make it worse. If you overshoot, let it be, and move on to the next thing. If you undershoot to the point of awkwardness, do the same.

On the other hand, if the rapport is going very well, sometimes you can upsize the ask. I remember a woman I sat on a charity board with who also worked for a large bank. I ran into her at a rubber chicken type of dinner for a nonprofit I'm involved with. When I followed up with an email the next day, I suggested catching up over lunch.

We had lunch and an unbelievable conversation. She's great. During that lunch, she says, "Gosh, I'd really like to help you. How can I help you?" That's the big moment. Don't hesitate to ask when that happens. I mentioned that there were a lot of people at the bank that I knew but didn't know well. It would be great if she could introduce me to those people.

I hadn't gone into that conversation expecting to ask for anything on that particular lunch, but we were vibing. I asked, and she went above and beyond. The relationship turned into a productive one for both of us.

LUNCH WITH A BILLIONAIRE

One of my mentors invited me to a lunch to introduce me to one of the people I idolize more than anyone else in the business world. This man is a true visionary and thought leader across many disciplines. He can buy and sell me a hundred times over and has more friends than anyone in the world. Needless to say, I was happy to show up to that lunch.

After that lunch, I now have the ability to follow up with touchpoints with that relationship. Perhaps someday something will come of that connection. Perhaps not. Either way I took away a lot of value from the discussion.

Power dynamics are important to connections. Working with peers is easy because you're both on similar power levels. Working at a very different power level is entirely another thing. We've all talked to a high school kid looking to get into business. When you help him or her, you're not looking for anything from him or her, right? You want to make the world a better place, and helping people makes you happy. You want them to make reasonable asks of you.

Conversely, when the power dynamic is inverted, you may want to make reasonable asks of the person you're with. You wouldn't ask to play video games with Bill Gates. However, it may make sense to ask how he got involved in a charity he supports. I generally don't ask for money or an introduction. Rather, I ask the person about their life, or for something they can provide on the spot without special effort. If they specifically inquire how they can help me, I say yes or no as feels right. Otherwise I put them in my mental bank of people I know and continue to follow up.

The currency that's being traded when you're helping people from a dramatic power imbalance is different than it is in a peer relationship. Helping someone's career and building communities is the right thing to do. It makes you feel good. Similarly, when you're in a position to make a reasonable ask of someone much more senior than you, if they like you, go for it. You're giving them an opportunity to feel good.

I OFTEN DON'T ASK

In a situation with a clear power differential, like Jack and the VP, I will ask in a non-pressuring way because it's more awkward not to ask and it gives people a chance to feel good. Other times, like with the billionaire, I won't ask because not asking will make me stand out. In a situation with peers, however, I normally don't ask, or at least don't ask right away.

Everything being equal, I'd much rather invest in the relationship. I'd rather connect, and help. I make a point of being the first to ask, "How can I help you?" Treating people well, with the right attitude, is essential to my philosophy of business.

A lot of people are so focused on what they can get out of

a situation that it sours the relationship. The point of life is people, right? I spend the time establishing rapport and helping people. I put relationship cash in the bank as generously as I can before I ever think about taking anything out. I expect the universe to take care of me in return and it does.

Results come out of peer relationships naturally, in their own timing, as long as people know what I do. (We'll talk more about how to move a relationship through the business cycle in the next chapter.) I'm looking to build win-win relationships that truly benefit everyone. I don't like one-way streets, and I'm not looking to win at the expense of anyone.

I want to be able to help people in their lives in a way that feels fundamentally balanced. That's not to say I won't help the high school or college kid, for the sake of it, and for the good feelings I get out of it. In the end, however, I would rather err on the side of generosity than selfishness. I don't want to be the guy taking. I want to be the guy building relationships that uplift everyone.

This philosophy has made my career. It feels good, and it's also gotten me unbelievable results. When you take care of people, people take care of you.

LIMITS TO GENEROSITY

I won't belabor the point, but I also don't do business with people who are always takers and who never give. I call these people one-way streets. If someone feels like a one-way street, that's a street I won't go down forever.

I give generously, but not endlessly. If it feels like I'm always helping and never get anything in return (even if just sincere gratitude), it doesn't feel good.

How do I decide when to walk away? If I wince when I get a call from someone, it's a signal to me that it might be time to get out of the relationship. When they call and I want to talk to them, that feels good.

Strategic relationship building must be good for everyone.

BE INTENTIONAL

Do keep an eye on what you want in any given relationship. Don't ask for a pitch if you want an ongoing relationship. However, don't spend so much time on trust building that you miss out on business opportunities.

Be mindful. Is the purpose of the interaction to establish a level of rapport and trust? Lean into that. Is the purpose of the interaction to really understand someone's business more? Ask many questions. Is the point to talk about possibly working together on a specific project? Settle into that conversation with your full attention. Have a goal going into each of those meetings.

Do your homework, understand where you stand in power dynamics, and be generous with help. You want people to get used to relying on you and calling you for help. You want to be reliable and consistent in your helpfulness. When a business opportunity arises, if people think of you as those things, they'll call you for that opportunity, too.

Be helpful. Follow up, and continue to follow up. Also keep your eye on your big picture goals, however. Why are you doing this? I'm guessing in the end you want to help yourself, your career, and help someone else. Act in such a way to support those goals.

This system will never work if you're running it solely off a spreadsheet. Interject what's driving you. Tune in to why you're doing what you're doing, and let your intention tell you what to do next.

EXTENDING YOUR NETWORK

You build bridges when you are human, authentic, and focused on being of service. You build bridges one girder at a time, slowly and carefully moving through the business cycle of relationships.

When you build relationships the right way, being focused on helpfulness, you create allies and advocates to represent you to the world. You create people who show up for you as you show up for them. You grow a community.

One of the most helpful things you can do for a person is to extend your network to them. If that person needs a car guy, introduce them to your car guy. If the person needs a tailor, introduce them to yours.

If you know me, and I have a guy I share, then by the transitive property of guys, you now have a guy, too.

Chapter Seven

THE TRANSITIVE PROPERTY OF GUYS

Jim is a relatively recent friend of mine. For lack of a better term, he's a fixer. He gets hired to help other people navigate serious problems going on in their lives, careers, and businesses. His job is both similar to and different from mine.

Jim's depth and breadth of relationships is so remarkable that he's the person I call when I don't know who else to call. He's a walking, talking Rolodex. For example, I was working on a real estate project where we suddenly had to have a bloodhound to sniff something up in the backyard.

(I've never needed a bloodhound before or since. That said, we had a piece of real estate and some rumors that a former affiliated person had buried various things, including money, on the property. I decided to take a look, on the theory that where there's smoke, there might be fire. Of course, the question then is "did you find anything?" I am appalled to say the answer is yes. However, we did need a bloodhound, and reasonably fast.)

Two phone calls, and Jim found someone who recommended someone who had a bloodhound for hire. Such is the weirdness and breadth of Jim's relationships. Just by knowing Jim you automatically have lots of ways to help people in your network. You benefit greatly, because he's your one phone call.

Jim has spent the last several decades of his life helping other people. Now, he's in the middle of the biggest deal of his life. It's a big, complex real estate deal that needs specific resources from different parts of the government. He'll need shipping help, logistics help, land use rights, transportation, and every obscure permit you can think of. None of these are items you can find in the Yellow Pages. There are only seven areas in the world with circumstances comparable to this one, and as a result the deal could make wild amounts of money—if he can make it happen on time.

Jim is probably one of a dozen people in the world who could pull this off. He's spent a lifetime building social capital, and he's cashing it all in. Lawyers, real estate, railroad people, politicians, shipping experts, businesspeople, advertising experts—all of these people were less than two degrees of separation away from Jim already. When he raised his hand and said, "Hey, guys, I need help," a flood of people showed up.

When Jim needed a specific person to find out an obscure detail about pulling a railroad tie, he made a phone call. He didn't have to go through the whole rigamarole of finding that person independently. He knew a guy who knew a guy. He knew a guy who vouched for him, and the railroad tie issue was solved.

Seeing Jim's network show up for him is inspiring. It will take an army to make this deal happen, but Jim has an army. In some ways, Jim is an army. His helpfulness has earned him a long line of people waiting to be helpful in return, and he stands to gain an insane amount of money as a result.

Jim is a perfect example of the strength of a lifetime's worth of building a network of guys. You cannot buy what he has. You can only build it. That said, *you can* share it. By having Jim as part of my ecosystem, and being helpful in return, I have Jim's army available to me when I need it. As he has my army in return.

THE TRANSITIVE PROPERTY OF GUYS

I have a guy, you might say, and he has a guy. So, by the transitive property of guys, I have a stadium full of guys ready and able to help.

Put another way, if I have a tailor, and my friend needs a tailor, she can call me for a recommendation. I have a guy, and now she has a guy. That's what I mean by the transitive property of guys.

Jim didn't know a bloodhound guy, or a railroad tie guy. He did, however, know someone to call who *would* know a bloodhound guy and a railroad tie guy, and that was just as good. As you expand your network, your guys will know guys, and your reach will grow exponentially.

(Remember the beginning of the book, when we talked about what I mean by the term "guy?" Men, women, and nonbinary people are all included. The language just feels too long and too cold when I say, "useful and competent person who I know and trust and like." "My guy," to me, implies something similar while also being affectionate and lighthearted. I have lots of guys in my life. Some of them happen to be women.)

If I know Guy A and Guy B, they're both my guys, but they don't know each other except through me. I am the glue between those relationships. Without me they're not able to help each other, and with me, they are. Communities are built through those kinds of connections, so it's worth your time to have a lot of guys. Networks pay dividends.

You might need a legal guy, a butcher guy, a banker, a tailor, or a mechanic guy. You might be somebody's tennis guy or consulting guy. You might offer a connection to school fundraiser guys. By knowing more guys, your network gains access to their guys in turn.

The larger your network, the more likely it is you'll be able to pick up the phone and find a bloodhound on short notice. Also, the more likely it is that you'll have a good experience doing everyday business.

You interact with people every day. When your friend goes to Starbucks, you might tell her to ask for Renee because she's really cool and always hooks you up with an extra shot of caramel. Or "talk to Ralph at the barber's because he's really good at making you feel warm and heard if you're having a bad day." Even if you don't know them well, Renee and Ralph are your guys.

You already have guys. As you continue to build relationships, you'll get many more—and you'll want to get guys deliberately when you can.

TALK ABOUT YOUR GUY

Remember how your kindergarten teacher taught you to share? Do that when it comes to your guys.

Talk about the tailor you love, the accountant who went

above and beyond for you, the girl who makes the best sand-wiches in the city. Talk about him or her any time it feels natural. Share your love of their services widely. It feels good, and you get to help a friend. What in the world can be bad about that?

Some people worry that sharing the name of your accoun-tant will make your guy get too busy to take good care of you anymore. That's rarely ever a problem, and the fear makes your guy miss out. If someone is doing a great job for you and you're happy with them, helping them build their business is the right thing to do. It feels natural and warm. Refusing to help them feels miserly. Who are we to try to limit what other people can do?

Rather than limit, use your network to actively help others get new opportunities. Otherwise, the next time you go to your guy, he might not be there anymore.

LISTEN

Listen when people talk, and pay attention. It sound obvious, but really—are you listening? Is the person just talking for the sake of talking, or are they looking for help? If the latter, then kindly ask if you can offer help. Only if they say yes should you offer up the name of your guy. Also, listen to what they need, or say they need. If someone wants help finding a preschool, don't offer a tutor.

I'll reemphasize *listening* to what people need. I know several people who are constantly trying to help people who don't want help. They constantly say that they have guys, even when no one asks, and come across as annoying, pushy, and boastful. Sometimes they offer the wrong things and make the conversation all about themselves to the point that it turns me off. The behavior feels "name-droppy" and negative. You don't want to be that guy.

Further, you don't want to be the guy that says you have guys when you don't, in fact, have guys. (Notice the three "guys" in one sentence, maybe for the first time in literary history!) If you say you have a guy, make damned sure you actually have that guy. Otherwise, you're an empty suit. Don't overreach on extending your guy. It's easier to clarify later than to overextend.

For example, you might say, "You have to go see my guy at the tailor shop. He's behind the suit store on Hollywood Boulevard, his name is Alex, and he's amazing. I'm pretty sure he has no idea what my name is, but if you tell him you're buddies with the guy that drives that blue Toyota that likes his pants tailored this way, he'll definitely take good care of you."

Listen and ask. Regardless of what people want, you'll look respectful and supportive. When they want help, you can be their helper. If they say, "no thanks, I've got this," you'll know to take them at their word. Either way you'll have put relationship capital in the bank and earned a good measure of trust.

Half of life—and this system—is listening to people.

CONNECT PEOPLE

Using your network for other people becomes one of the most powerful things you can do, particularly once you're senior in your field or established in your community. Talk up your tailor—he deserves it. However, think beyond just your guy. Often you'll meet two people who could benefit from each other, and you can connect them. Always do it if you can—connections gain you goodwill, and helping makes you feel good.

I introduce people with the context of how I know them. That gives an opportunity for people to know when I'm vouching for someone versus merely introducing someone I've just met. You might say, "I think you should talk to Mike. I've worked with Mike on this before, and he knows what he's doing. Probably worth a shot. Calls are free." Be low pressure and easy, with a genuinely helpful attitude.

What you want to avoid is overpromising. A lukewarm email can serve the purpose, establish goodwill, but not promise anything if I don't know someone. For example, I talked to a guy last week who interviewed for a job with us. While he wasn't ultimately a good fit for us, he seemed like he'd be a great fit for a company I was working with. Since they were hiring, I connected the two.

I have code words in my emails in these situations. If I say, "Talk to Shah, he's one of my best friends. I've known him since I was three," I mean he's literally one of my best friends and you should take very good care of him. In contrast, for a passing acquaintance I might say, "Shah, meet John. John, meet Shah. I ran into Shah at a conference, and he sounds like he's hiring specialists. John is a friend of a colleague and sounds like he has that exact specialty. I think you guys should talk." In that case, everyone knows I don't know much about either of them.

I probably send three emails a day connecting people. It becomes a convenient way to stay top of mind while being helpful, and it makes me feel good. I'm guessing it's also been terribly good for my career.

SOCIAL IS IMPORTANT, TOO

Keep in mind that connections should go beyond business.

Every day you're out in the community talking to people: your dentist, the guy at the farmer's market who sells berries, or the other parents at the school drop off. Sometimes you'll find people with common interests, and you should connect them. Is Marla into kite surfing? She should talk to Linda, who also loves kite surfing. You could suggest they go kite surfing together, if that feels right, or for Linda to introduce Marla, who is new in town, around the kite surfing community locally. The sky's the limit.

Everyone is social on some level, and we can all use help and connections in that arena, too. Early in your career, before you have the established business network, social may in fact be your best arena. If you're the person who knows where to get the best artisan pickles, you could be valuable to the CEO, who's really into artisan pickles, or better, the CEO's daughter who's *super* into artisan pickles. Your interests could be what connect you to the person who can transform your life.

You'll be surprised at how many people with whom you can build warm relationships over jazz or football or *Game of Thrones*. You'll be surprised at how many people you can help with ideas or connections or simply fun events.

Occasionally social connections can turn into business, as it has for my business a few times. You never know who is connected to whom. However, even if no one ever helps you in the business world, you'll have built great relationships based on jazz or football or *Game of Thrones*. Those relationships have inherent value and make everyone's lives better.

Now that I'm more senior in my career, I tend to use my network to help others primarily on the business side. Several of my more junior guys, however, do very well helping on the social side. Today's junior accountant and golf buddy might very well be a full partner in ten years. He'll take your call if you're his long-term golf buddy.

Even more importantly, however, you'll have had the benefit of a fun golf buddy in the meantime.

PEOPLE GROW

Twelve years ago, I met Matt. He worked at a huge corporation with hundreds of thousands of people, and he ranked perhaps twenty-five-thousandth. I liked him, and he liked me. There was no business reason to be friends. We tried to help each other, but it didn't often work out. It didn't matter. We were great friends.

Over twelve years, Matt has elevated his career to be in the top hundred of this behemoth organization. I founded a company. The kind of seniority and power we have now was not even in the cards when we first met. Because we've grown together and developed deep trust together over a decade of friendship, I can call Matt and get a meeting without notice. He can do the same with me. We are peers at a different level.

The main advantage of building the relationship over time is that there's trust. There's no smell of opportunism or using.

We were two people trying to help each other out (which we did many times). He has people calling on him from my field *all the time* now. He often doesn't take those calls, because I'm his guy and I've been consistent.

If I came to Matt from my position now, to the senior position he holds, it would be a very different conversation. I don't know that he would take a meeting. Ten years of amalgamated trust, however, adds up to a solid relationship that can bear a lot of weight. We shortcut a lot of posturing by virtue of starting a friendship when we were kids.

IN THE ERA OF THE INTERNET

In the Information Age, whenever you want to know about something, you can do a Google search. Seconds from now, you'll find any number of people online willing to tell you about that thing—whether they actually have any expertise on the subject or not. I sometimes wonder if the pre-90s era protected us from some of the scammers. A world that vouched for experts seems easier to navigate.

I know maybe twenty-five pastrami sandwich places that have some version of "Best Pastrami Sandwich on Earth" on their sign. I've always found that funny. What authority crowned *this* place the best on the planet? Did that person really try every pastrami sandwich before declaring it? Did they ever go to Langer's, clearly the best one by far?

The internet, and the tools available cheaply on the internet, have created millions, maybe billions of websites that are the equivalent of the "Best Pastrami on Earth." You can get good, cheap art; good copywriting; AI tools to build your website; and a number of other things supposedly the best in the business. Maybe they are. Maybe they aren't. That's one of the hard parts of being alive today. There's so much information, and no good filter to sort out what's real.

Fortunately, people work the same in the twenty-first century as they did back then. By looking for experts through your network rather than online, you're cutting out the posturing and BS. The rest of the network knows and trusts your new guy. They've seen him be a good guy. You get well taken care of.

When Jim needed a railroad tie pulled, he didn't have to ask Google. He didn't have to wade through twenty engineering firms from Peru that looked like they knew what they were doing. He didn't have to figure out how to vet any of them. Instead, he picked up the phone and got an expert in an afternoon.

You probably won't need a bloodhound or a railroad tie problem solved any time soon, but you'll need something, or your friends will. "Do you know a good butcher? Do you know a good place to get things engraved? Where should I get my pants tailored?" Try Googling any of those questions and see the mess of results that you get back. How do you choose? When you have a guy, you don't have to hunt-and-peck through Google, and—as importantly—neither does your friend. You'll also get a guy who actually knows what she is doing, every time.

THE NEW NETWORK

There's a lot of criticism of old boy's networks, where small, exclusive groups of mostly men sit around giving business to people in their small group and only their small group. For all its surface similarity, the system I'm teaching you isn't that. If anything, I'm teaching you how to build a network of peers—and guys—who will help you grow beyond the limitations you might be facing now.

The old boy's network in some ways is a desperate attempt to try to maintain control of a world that doesn't need to be controlled so strictly. What I am teaching you becomes a mechanism to storm the gates and return control to everybody. We're flipping the script on exclusivity and making this all about inclusivity. The person that makes that "flip" is you. You're the pivot point to make something exclusive into something inclusive. Building communities means building your own boy's and girl's network that you can choose to make more inclusive, more open, and more effective.

By building connections with a wide group of peers and

guys and growing together, we have an opportunity to bring networks into the twenty-first century. Now rooms have more kinds of people in them. The transitive property of guys, the communities we build, and the new guy's and gal's networks become richer and more viable because there are more people in the room.

As you build your network, try to be more deliberate about seeking out women, if your network is short on women, and the same for people with a diversity of backgrounds and experiences. I'm involved in a group we call the Eagles (the story behind the name is long and not that interesting). We get together once a month to try to help each other out, like a mastermind group or personal board of directors. When I was asked to join this group, I was concerned that nobody in the group was "in my business" so it would be a waste of time. The person who invited me said to give it a chance and that everyone said that at first. Sure enough, I couldn't have been more wrong. The diversity of backgrounds, careers, stories, and perspectives makes the Eagles the single most important group I'm in outside of my family. More diversity means more ability to help.

You can't always control who organically grows into your network, but you can take opportunities to invite interesting and competent, diverse people into your network. The network is better, in general, when there are more, different people in the room. Everyone has a story. Everyone has value. You may be the launching pad they need to let their rocket fly.

THE MULTIPLIER EFFECT

I've always taken great joy in introducing one part of my network to another. I get to sit in the middle of the flywheel, helping everyone around me, seeing everyone be happy. It's an amazing feeling. I've benefitted greatly over the years from other people introducing me, and I'm always happy to do the same for someone else. People I like and who do great work deserve having their businesses grow.

A healthy network is inherently valuable to everyone within it. The larger the network, if it's healthy, the better for everyone involved. If I know three people, and they each know three people, my network is now nine. I am nine times more likely to get a referral than I was before, for the price of having met three people.

What's interesting about networks is what I call the multiplier effect. The three becomes nine example is easy, but the reality is exponentially greater. If you meet only fifty people per year (less than one per week!), and you keep up with them, you'll know fifty people. If, however, as usually happens with humans, each of them already knows just fifty people—a small number—at the end of the year you'll have increased your reach to fill a mid-sized high school gymnasium.

I'll say it again to reemphasize. If you meet less than one person per week and follow up appropriately, you'll have a minimum of 2,500 new people in your network at the end of the year. If you talk to 150 new people per year, not even three per week, and follow up, you'll have over twenty-two thousand people in your room. That's bigger than (most) high school football stadiums in Texas.

Even if what you do is obscure, someone in that room will need your services—and likely several someones. By the transitive property of guys, you'll be the "guy" to enough people to fill a large town. If you follow up and stay top of mind, your business will thrive.

WARM INTRODUCTIONS SMOOTH THE ROAD

Cars are arguably a commodity market. You can buy the same Ford at one dealership that you can at another. As a result, you might be tempted to think that any salesman would do, and relationships wouldn't matter. You'd be wrong, of course.

One day I was walking to lunch when I bumped into Aram, a business buddy of mine. I see him frequently, and for some reason that day I remembered that he knows a lot of car dealers. I told him that my wife and I were in the market for a new car. We knew exactly what we wanted. Did he know any dealers who could help us get it? We like to support friends or friends of friends if we can.

Forty-five minutes later Aram introduced me to Patrick and told Patrick to take good care of me. It was the single best car buying experience of my life.

My wife and I showed up the next day, signed three pieces of paper, and we were done. Everything was packed and the car was ready to drive off the lot that minute. I was so grateful I bought the guy a bottle of wine. I'd been braced for a miserable day of haggling at the dealership, for the razzle-dazzle dance of going back to the back room and negotiating all day. Instead, it was effortless.

With a warm introduction, there was no hassle. No one had to size anyone up. We already knew where we stood. We treated each other like grown adults worthy of warmth and respect.

In business, this happens all the time. A friend of mine needed a lawyer quickly this week for a project he was working on. I made a warm introduction to the guy, with the key "code words" that we've discussed earlier in the book. In this case: he's a good friend, I use him, my firm uses him, and so forth. My friend retained my lawyer friend in less than forty-five minutes. There was no friction. There was no shopping around, wining and dining, spam emails, marketing departments, or boring conferences. Two friends and twenty-seven words, and they were both off to the races.

What's true with lawyers, dealerships, and banks is true

everywhere. We relax with people with know, and people our people trust are almost as good. Warm introductions make everything easier.

Use your network to help others like Aram did, and like I did yesterday. Make the world a better place one introduction at a time.

WIN-WIN VERSUS WIN-LOSE

Some people have a philosophy of looking for the win at the expense of everyone else. They feel like the world is a pie and any piece you have is a piece I don't. I disagree strongly with this philosophy. Building win-win relationships creates much more value over time.

When you do business with people you trust, it feels warm and good. Patrick told me that I got the best price he could absolutely give me. "You can call around. You can verify what I'm telling you. You're a friend of a friend, and I gave you literally the best price I can." I knew enough about the car and the industry to know he was telling me the truth, and as a result I'd send anyone I knew to buy a car from him.

When you build win-win relationships, you don't have to worry about little things. If you get a chip in your paint, when the car salesperson feels valued and appreciated, he likely gets it fixed for you for free. On the other hand, if you nickel and dime people to death to find the win-lose, you have to watch every detail. You're having to overcome a lot of ill will to get anything done, and you're definitely paying for that paint job.

In business, this happened yesterday. We were going to retain a law firm for very specialized thing, and we reached out to someone through one of my guys. To be fair, my guy "barely knew him," so I was warned. This person clearly wasn't aligned with my philosophy. We could have spent hundreds of thousands of dollars with him, but after a few intro phone calls, we get an invoice before we signed an engagement letter. The money wasn't much, but sending the invoice for a consult call felt so tacky that it made me angry. We'll pay it, but here's what happened: A) He lost my business for the larger project forever. B) I talked to the referring guy and told him what happened, and so the lawyer also lost his business or any of his guys' business. And C) my guy called the guy that referred him, and the lawyer lost his business. To sum up, for a few thousand dollars this lawyer may have lost hundreds of times that in business. Don't be an asshole. Treat people as you want to be treated. Or you'll find what goes around comes around. The network effect can work against you as easily as for you.

When you build win-wins, on the other hand, you can come back and do business over and over, and people help you.

It's a better way to work. Take the time to really look for the win-wins and to do business with people you like. Even here, be helpful.

Be the person other people are glad to see coming.

BE GENEROUS

Don't be miserly with your network. Share your connections generously, with an attitude of helpfulness. You'll create a powerful spiderweb of helping.

Jim spent years finding ways to help people by connecting one end of his network with another. I myself have reached out to Jim and asked him to help me with a project, and he made exactly the right introduction. When Jim needed help in turn, then, I and everyone else in the network showed up. He was able to pull off an impossible deal.

When Aram helped me find a car salesman, I had a very pleasant experience. Aram helped his guy. His guy helped me. I made Aram look good in front of his guy and brought his guy some money. Because I asked for help, and Aram shared his network, we were all uplifted.

Build your network beyond people in your field. Find stringers for your tennis racket and the right people to buy cars from. Find a bank guy, a tax guy, and every other role you come across. Then connect them to the rest of your network. When you share your guys, everyone benefits.

BE PATIENT

Very rarely, you might see a business stranger across the room and fall in business love with them. Perhaps less rarely, if you've been hacking relationships for a long time like I have, you might be able to skip some of the courtship steps and make a good deal faster than the average. For the most part, however, relationships take time to develop.

Overnight sales take months or years to develop. Be calm, continue to develop strategic relationships, and trust that good things will happen.

They always do.

Chapter Eight

PATIENCE, PADAWAN

Keren is an executive coach. She happens to be my executive coach and has done extraordinary things for me. Keren was an executive before she became a coach. She's been very open about the fact that she had several personal crises that led her to self-help and then to what she's doing now. She started helping herself, she says, and eventually moved to helping anyone else who would listen.

Keren believes in action, so when in doubt, she tries something and sees what happens. In her own business, she has tried networking, Instagram posts, and even YouTube content. Eventually the work she put in began to compound. She began to meet her first handful of clients and served them.

Eventually she became so successful she was able to quit her other job and focus entirely on executive coaching. She created additional content to serve more of her people's needs, and that led to speaking engagements at prestigious events.

Then she started getting asked to speak on TV and podcasts. She went on the *TODAY Show* and *Good Morning America*. She went on so many podcasts that she eventually started her own. Now she's doing TED talks.

Two years later, Keren is working with Gwyneth Paltrow. Her endgame when she started wasn't to be sitting next to Oprah, though I believe that's going to happen for her. Instead, she stepped out. She started acting, and her actions compounded.

One relationship turned into four relationships, which turned into more. The more people who Keren was able to serve, the more she was introduced to others, and the further her reach extended. She was conscientious and deliberate about spending her time and energy on productive things and productive relationships, and over time, she built a business.

Keren is good at relationships. She's not afraid to ask. Somehow, however, she's never annoying or weird. She's brassy and charming, and she's asking from a place of wanting to help more people. She's putting good vibrations out into the universe, and it feels authentic.

Keren asks out of a sense of integrity. She's asked me, "I would love to be able to help other people you know and other clients of yours so I can keep doing this. Is there anyone you can introduce me to?" Keren has already moved through the entire business cycle with me. We're friends. I want to help her. I believe in what she's doing, and so when she asks me to introduce her in the hopes of helping other people, I want to help.

Keren's attitude is such that I believe she could do the same thing to a person at one of her conferences and have the same result. When you have the right attitude, good things happen.

BE LIKE ANNE

Anne sold auto insurance for a large insurance company. Everywhere she went, she made friends. She'd ask if she could run someone's numbers to see if she could save them money on their auto insurance, and she meant it. Sure, she'd make more money if she sold a policy, but her attitude was helping the person in front of her.

Anne also gave out her cell phone number to anyone who bought an auto insurance policy from her in person. She told everyone, "if you get into an accident, call me. I'll listen and I'll walk you through what you do to file a claim and be taken care of. Any time of day or night, you get into an accident, call me."

I doubt Anne had to take more than a few calls per year, but her attitude sold policies. People liked her, and they were happy to stay with the company if it meant they could call Anne. Because she had an attitude of helping, she was a highly successful salesperson.

People felt like they had personal relationships with her and introduced her to their networks. Anne makes it into her clients' 150. She becomes an important person in their lives by being helpful and having the right attitude. That has made her business.

RELAX AND TRUST

You'll get to the place where someone knows you, they understand what you do, and they like you. Now comes time to "let it happen." You hang around the net, so to speak, waiting for the puck to come in your direction. You stick around until the inevitable day comes when the person or someone they know needs your services.

I'll repeat the chorus to the song we've been singing this whole book, in reverse: if they don't remember you're alive, why would they call you? So wait patiently while reminding the person periodically that you're alive.

While you're waiting, help people. They'll help you. When the puck comes your way, you'll be ready for it.

It's worth restating at this point that we don't expect the

same people we help will be necessarily the ones who show up to help us. That's not how the universe works. Instead, we relax and trust that good things will happen—they usually do.

When we put ourselves in the right place at the right time strategically, good things happen more often. We don't have to watch the clock because we know that we'll be okay.

LET ME INTRODUCE YOU TO MY UNCLE

I met Aaron, an investment banker, when I was working on a large case for a company a handful of years ago. We really hit it off; we were the same age, had the same sense of humor, and shared a lot of the same interests. Aaron was on my level. If I was targeting peers, he was my guy. Even better, we both liked each other.

The case, as it happened, centered on a legal trial. Everything about it was tough. I ended up testifying as an expert in federal court, and opposing counsel was raking me over the coals. If you ever have to do anything like that, be aware you won't be allowed to talk to anyone on your team over lunch. You're a witness.

Aaron wasn't on my team at that point, and he invited me to lunch. We went to a different restaurant than everyone else and ate bad salads by the courthouse. We weren't allowed to talk about anything remotely similar to the case, but I needed to talk. He showed up on a very human level for me. We talked about our families. We talked about what we like to do in the summer. We talked about everything except the one thing we already knew about each other. When lunch broke and I went back on the stand, I'd made a friend.

We stayed in touch. He's in New York, and I'm in Los Angeles, and whenever he comes to Los Angeles he'll reach out. We end up talking about bread, of all things. He loves to bake, and I love anything related to food. He was into artisan bakeries around New York, and claimed there wasn't any good bread in Los Angeles, so I went out and found good bread for him when he was in town. We got bread, and built a friendship.

About a year and a half later, I was visiting New York, and Aaron and I were chitchatting on the way to another bakery. He told me in an oddly serious voice that he should introduce me to his uncle. His uncle was going through a lot of the things I was talking about and could use some help. He'd be happy to introduce me, he said.

It turns out that Aaron's uncle is the CEO of a huge company. I had no idea. I'd been going for bread with this investment banker friend because it was fun and I always need another business contact, but suddenly that turned into an introduction with a major company and a mentor for me. I couldn't have set that up if I'd tried. Nor would Aaron have introduced me if I'd gone in with the wrong attitude. People trying to use people end up putting off a gross vibe. When I showed up to build a relationship I enjoyed over bread, on the other hand, I got an authentic connection that helped me.

Incidentally, this is a two-way street. I've called Aaron on three or four potential projects and vice versa. From the sublime to the mundane, we have been able to help each other out, because of the relationship we've developed. Bread and business go well together.

When you go into relationships with authenticity, good things happen. However, they often happen randomly and over time. Sometimes the dentist can be more helpful to you in your business career than the person who works at the *right firm*. You shouldn't be so targeted in your relationships that you miss out on the random good the universe has for you. Be open, and be a good person.

RELATIONSHIPS ARE BUILT LIKE BRIDGES

If I had tried to ask for an introduction from Aaron, it may not have happened. However, I can tell you it definitely wouldn't have happened if I'd asked Aaron for it the second time we'd gone for bread. The relationship couldn't withstand that kind of weight and, like a bridge overstrained, it would have collapsed.

It takes time to build bridges, beam by beam, girder by girder. Similarly, it takes time to construct a relationship with interactions, vulnerability, and trust. Aaron and I built a friendship out of dozens of trustworthy interactions. When it was time, he felt that the relationship could support the weight of a familial introduction to someone he admired.

Once bridges are built, they can support the weight of huge numbers of cars, trucks, and people driving across. Don't take a new bridge for granted, however. If you try to drive a car over a half-finished suspension bridge, you'll end up in the ocean. If you try to over-ask of a new relationship, you'll destroy it completely.

Be patient and focus on building the bridge with a good attitude.

BE WEIRD

Also noteworthy from that story is the way Aaron and I bonded. Connecting with people often happens around the weird interests you have in common. It can feel absurd. You can't just go for artisan bread with any person on the golf course, however. You're going to get bread with a guy just as weird (or interesting) as you. Everyone has things that are unique about them. If they don't, they're a robot, and they're boring. It's like the last line on a resume, the "other interests" line. I am more likely to ask in an interview about your card-house hobby than which finance class you took in college. If you're at the interview, you're qualified. I'd like to get to know you on a human level.

Have you seen *Good Will Hunting?* There's a scene when Will asks his love interest (Skylar) if she wants to go out for caramels because it's just as arbitrary and social as getting coffee. For me, I go get bread, or ramen, or whatever else. The arbitrariness makes it memorable. The randomness makes it fun.

Be weird. Be fully weird and interested in the (noncontroversial) things that light you up. Talk about those things at work, around the water cooler or at mixers. Talk about your interests, and you'll often find people will connect with you specifically for those interests. Go crazy for football, or bread, or *Game of Thrones*. Connect over caramels, or love of obscure Greek theater. Be weird, and enjoy the people who will be weird with you.

Go find your artisan bread relationship. It'll be fun, and it might just pay off one day. In the meantime, though, you'll have had extraordinary bread and good company.

CONCLUSION

I'm in a business education group where we each take turns creating events for the others to attend and learn something interesting. When it was my turn to host, I decided that my event would be centered on security. We were having terrible active shooter events going on in the world, and the topic seemed germane.

I've learned over the years to talk about whatever I'm doing in my life at that moment to my network, especially if it's something interesting like a security education event. Having something to talk about is valuable in the quest to remain top of mind, and every now and then someone will be able to help me with what I'm doing. That day I was talking about my plans to a guy we'll call James.

Not very far into the conversation, James laughed. "You know what I do for a living, right?" I replied with my vague understanding that he was in the computer business. "No, actually, I run an international security company, and we do trainings for people on cyber crime and physical security."

Lucky break! It's always great to speak with an expert on a subject I'm interested in. I asked James if he had any advice for me on putting together the event. He laughed and told me he had a full staff of trainers who go to multinational companies to teach on the subject all the time. "I'm happy to lend some resources to your event."

For the price of meeting the right person in my network and talking to him about an interesting project, I got a trainer to speak to my group for free that otherwise would have cost me thousands.

As I've implemented strategic relationship building in my life, and as I talk about my interests to my network, these kinds of coincidences happen for me more often than you'd think. When you get people in a room talking, weird and wonderful things happen.

They will for you, too—if you'll do the work.

CONNECTION

I've noticed that the energy is different when I'm talking on the phone than it is when I show up in person. It's different shaking hands than it is sending an emoji fist bump. People are social creatures, and we're wired first and foremost to be social in direct proximity.

I've taken body language classes before, and the foundational fact is that communication is 90 percent nonverbal. Body language, tone, pace, inflection, and even how we gesture with our hands all impact how we understand the words that are said. Reading sentences on a page carries with it an infinitesimal amount of the information we'd get from a person sitting across from us. A face means so much more than a string of words.

Whenever I see ground wars and firefights online, on social media, on text, and everywhere else, I wonder, was something interpreted wrong? Or are people just more brutal when they don't have to look at someone's face? If we were all sitting around a campfire, I don't think many of those same conversations would happen. Too much is lost in translation.

This book, in part, is a call to go back to the kinds of in-person relationship building that humans have used for centuries. In the business world, it's much harder to say no to someone's face than over email. It's much harder to ignore someone in the same room—when you ask them what they think in person, they'll tell you something. Online, they might just keep scrolling, especially when they're bombarded with thousands of pings a day. We're all tired online.

Connection is critically important for humans, and connection happens primarily in person. Text messages, emails, LinkedIn messages, etc., are fine and powerful in their way, but they work best when they build upon and supplement an in-person relationship.

Even digital communication, however, should always be personal. We don't send spam. We don't tell people how great we or the companies we work for are. We reach out with "Hey did you see the game last night?" or "Thinking of you and hope you're doing well." A touchpoint is a personal contact.

Humans are social creatures. We need connection. Everything I've taught you in this book is centered on that one key fact.

STRATEGIC RELATIONSHIP BUILDING

You talk to people every day, and you build relationships, even shallow ones, naturally through the day to day interactions with people in your world. Why leave the most important building blocks of your life to chance?

Strategic relationship building, in contrast, means actively trying to build relationships. It's mindfully reaching out to five people a day or five people a week, consistently. It's creating touchpoints and being consistent and dependable with your follow-ups. It's building a life full of relationships, and guys, and connecting people within your network.

This system isn't difficult, but it does take intentionality. Some people create a great network on accident, but I think most come from intention.

We've talked about not getting too precious with your communication. Don't spend the two weeks building Power-Points. Instead, spend those two weeks creating touchpoints and going out to lunch with people. Waiting to be perfect will kill your progress. Perfect is the enemy of the good, and consistency is far more important than perfection.

You can absolutely do this. It's your choice.

ADDING IN JOY

Relationships should be easy and fun. They're the connections you make in your day already, expanded and done on purpose. My theory is that every relationship you make *could* have been one that happened organically if you'd worked in the cubicle next door to someone. Adding intentionality merely makes it happen outside of proximity.

We all say, "Don't be a stranger," and, "Let's keep in touch." When you do the work to maintain and deepen relationships, you follow through on your word. Ninety-nine percent of people will say those things and then let the relationship go. You'll be the one who doesn't. That alone will grow into a competitive advantage.

You loved getting bread, drinking coffee, or going for drinks last time. Doing it again on a regular schedule isn't onerous. If anything, it adds joy to your life. Don't let yourself get too busy to maintain the relationships in your life and continue to add new ones. It will grow your life and your business at the same time.

Go through your notes every now and then, scroll through your contacts on your phone, or look through your contacts on your email. The most valuable asset any human being has is their relationships. Don't leave the outcome of your relationships to chance—nourish those interactions, however deep or shallow, and create circumstances that allow you to help one another.

These are the people who will make your life better. Treat them well.

BEING HELPFUL

When you're talking with people, be helpful. I'm not necessarily saying you actually do service work. You could, but it takes a lot of time. Being helpful is broader than that.

When you build relationships with touchpoints, presumably the people you're reaching will enjoy spending time with you, talking about something they like. Art, cooking, football, cats, etc., are things that tend to bring sparks of joy to all of our lives. When you talk about something pleasant or make someone feel heard, you're brightening both of your days.

Often people will ask for help, and you can actually help them. Or you can notice an area of their lives where you might be able to help and ask about it. If they're willing, you might introduce a person to your guy. You open up your heart, your Rolodex, and your resources for someone. You share the latest great taco place or introduce people to your tailor. You show up for people and make their lives better.

Over time, the relationship grows into something that feeds you, too.

STARTING NOW

Open up your phone—or your email—and find someone you haven't talked to in a long time. If you flick your finger up the contacts on your phone, the wheel will stop on a random name. Do you wish you'd seen that person more recently than you have?

I did this as I was writing this page, and my thumb stopped on Nick. I haven't talked to Nick in probably a year and a half, but every time I see him, I enjoy the hell out of the conversation. I always end up wondering why we don't get together every week.

I recall that Nick loves working out, triathlons, business, and flying small planes. So I might send him a message that sounds like this: "Hey man, I was working on a book and came across your name, and I wondered why we don't get together more often," or "I was talking to a buddy last night who just finished an Ironman and thought of you. Let's get lunch again."

I'd recommend you stop reading right now and spend a minute or two reaching out to a contact with a similar message. I'll be here when you get back.

CONTINUING THE PRACTICE

Did you reach out? Great. If not, seriously do that now.

Now, please.

Done? Great. We'll move on.

Once you've reached out to a contact, continue the trend. Make the goal of reaching out to a certain number of your contacts each week. Write that goal on your calendar as a reminder for Friday afternoon, and spend a little time then following up. If you make more touchpoints than your goal, that's great! My goal was thirty a week. It sounds like a lot, but it's really not much.

Don't neglect new contacts for old, however. Set up opportunities in your schedule to continue to meet new people. Remember those networking events with the terrible food? Sign up for one in your city soon. You might also want to join the local tennis club if you like tennis, for example.

Even if you're introverted (as I am somewhat), you can still go to one or two events per month. Schedule a recovery day or morning if you need to—introverted doesn't mean you're not social, just that you need some down time afterward. Just don't forget to follow up! Once you've made a good contact, you don't want to waste the opportunity.

GROW YOUR NETWORK IN-PERSON

Everybody eats lunch. Rather than taking your sandwich and eating at your desk, turn that time into productive relationship time. If everyone eats at the office, create an office lunch table. At conferences, take the meal breaks as opportunities to connect over food. Life in generally is better with community, and community happens easily over food.

Doesn't food taste better with other people there? Plus, you eat slower, which I think is good for you.

HAPPY PEOPLE MAKE CONNECTIONS

Every now and then I'll see another person with a large network and a happy life. He or she always finds a way to create touchpoints and follow up, whether by nature or artifice. People like this attract other people, almost like a force of gravity. One friend leads to another. One happiness builds on the next.

Whenever I see a person like this, I stop and pay attention. It's inspirational to see someone with a happy family, lots of fun stuff going on, many friends and friends of the family. None of that is built by accident. It affirms the reason I work so hard on touchpoints and helping. It reminds me why I practice strategic relationship building.

You can build that kind of life, too. It just takes deliberate effort, consistently executed over time.

YOUR BIGGEST ASSET

Studies show that the depth and breadth of your relationships are, in the end, what will make you happy. Even if you never received anything from your relationships other than a rich happy life, that would be enough. No one wants to be the richest lonely person in the graveyard. Building a career is important, but doing so in a way that leaves you lonely isn't satisfying. Why not build a life that gives you both at the same time?

Strategic relationship building has yielded huge dividends for me. It's brought real monetary value in my businesses and meaningful relationships into my life. You can do the same.

Whatever your service or career is, there is someone else in the world that does it. We are all fungible. What really separates us from the long list of competitors and creates value is what I call your book of business. If you ever leave your current job, your relationships go with you.

Companies often worry that their employees will steal their customer relationship data. Whenever we have to let someone go, however, it's the furthest thing from my mind. If the person we let go has a relationship with someone, I can follow up with that relationship, but if he doesn't know me from Adam, it doesn't matter. The relationship truly does belong to the person who made it.

When I'm interviewing people, on the other hand, of course I look for excellent skills. Want to know what gets me excited about a candidate, though? That same book of business. When a person shows up with a big bundle of relationship assets around her neck, it's a scarce commodity and intensely valuable.

Relationships are everyone's most important asset. At the end of the day, people do business with people.

TAKE CARE OF YOUR ASSETS

I think people understand how important maintaining your health is. You take care of your body by going to the gym, eating well, and drinking water. Maintaining relationships is just that critical and should be approached with just as much care. Treat your network with the care those relationships deserve.

If you don't bring water with you to the desert, you might not die in the time it takes you to explore and drive home. You'll feel very unpleasant, however, and your body will warn you not to do it again. Letting relationships go will similarly have consequences. Let them go long enough, and your social life—and that critical book of business—will die.

On the other hand, the more you invest in relationships, the more valuable they get. Like a Chia Pet, the more you tend relationships, feed them, and water them, the more they grow.

People don't start at one company and end there fifty years later anymore. The world changes too often, and the economy moves too quickly. What will separate you as you move from company to company is the same thing I look for senior people for my firm—that beloved relationship network. If you have it, you will thrive. If you don't, particularly in a service business, your skills alone may not be enough.

Why wouldn't you reach out and build relationships, given everything at stake? You have the time in the day, and the ability to accomplish everything you need. The habit feels good and makes other people feel good. Not to mention its long-term potential to make you more money and grow your career. The investment is so small—and the long-term payoff so big.

I repeat, why not?

A SIMPLE SYSTEM

In this book, I've shown you how to build strategic relationships on purpose. It's not hard—but it does take consistency and dedication over time. You can start today, but you'll gain the most if you follow through over the course of years.

Take small steps to make and keep connections. Craft touchpoints. Send them. Don't push; accept and enjoy light relationships with contentment. Follow up with people, and keep following up. Be a good human, be of service, and stay top of mind. Treat people well.

If you can send a hundred touchpoints this month, do. If you can only send two, however, two is better than zero. I sent thirty touchpoints a week to start my business, but you may only decide to do five. Send those five, and if you forget one week, send ten the next. Consistency matters more than perfection.

You can do this. So, do it.

ACKNOWLEDGMENTS

I'd like to thank the thousands and thousands of people who have met me for breakfast, coffee, lunch, dinner, drinks, and other meetings over the last twenty years. A lot of hot air has flown from these lips, and I'm glad someone was on the other side to hear it. This book and my career don't exist without you.

I would like to thank the entire Scribe Media team for your support. Thank you to Tucker, who made it less scary; to Kacy for her steady hand; to the graphics and copywriting people who made my vision happen; but mostly to Alex for her quick study, patience, time, and talent. You all are very impressive and made this whole process fun and exciting. Thank you. This book would literally not exist without you.

I'd like to thank Curtis for making the introduction. Curtis embodies this philosophy more than anyone I've ever met, and I consider him a mentor and inspiration as a result.

Thank you for introducing me to Ben, who introduced me to Tucker to get this thing going.

I'd also like to thank the investors in my failed startup around this idea, though I did not get it right in execution. You believed in me, so I hope to get the idea out another way and see if people will embrace it in book form. To my investors, I appreciate your support and friendship (or former friendship) and thank you sincerely for your vote of confidence and support.

Next I'd like to thank my coach and friend, Keren, for opening up my eyes to the possibilities. I've been someone who's been concerned with what other people think, and her encouragement to let my "Inner Larry" out is a big part of the inspiration to let go and go for it.

I'd also like to thank my colleagues for their support in getting our business to where it is, indulging my weirdness, and giving me the freedom to pursue this journey. The whole SierraConstellation Crew is a constant source of inspiration to me, and something I'm so proud to be part of.

My friends have also supported this. Yes, with some eye rolls and ribbing along the way, but I know you have my back. I appreciate the support and encouragement, particularly from the High Vibe Tribe and the Yazerkins.

I'd also like to thank the Eagles. Your support and inspiration makes me want to be a better person, and your friendship and camaraderie make it a fun journey. Thank you to all of you, past and present.

I want to thank my dad for always having a book in his hand when I was growing up, even if it was sometimes a romance novel. He helped foster the love of books and reading that I carry to this day. I also want to thank my late mother for emphasizing and sacrificing to get me a great education.

Thank you to my daughter, Dagny, for being someone I want to make proud. As fun as it is for me to write this, my favorite part may be seeing you tell people that I am also an author. It's a very fuzzy, warm feeling. I love you.

More than anyone, I want to thank my wife, Nichole. Nichole, you have seen a better version of me than I have from the beginning. You have single-handedly guided, steered, prodded, pushed, supported, corrected, allowed, and ultimately loved me in a way that has allowed me to be me. You have gotten me to where I am. Like everything, we are a practice, not an outcome. It's taken me a while to understand, but here we are, and I am grateful. I truly couldn't do this without you and your love and support. I love you.

ABOUT THE AUTHOR

LAWRENCE PERKINS founded what is now SierraConstellation Partners at age twenty-nine with few connections and very little capital. Lawrence grew SCP into a nationwide management consulting group serving nearly one hundred large companies in their times of most dire need. Today, Lawrence is a recognized industry leader who's spoken at major industry conferences and has been cited by the *Wall Street Journal,* the *New York Times,* CNN, CNBC, and the *Washington Post.* Outside of work, Lawrence has built a remarkable life with his wife and daughter that includes interests ranging from reading and writing to singing and dancing to cooking and running.

CPSIA information can be obtained
at www.ICGtesting.com
Printed in the USA
LVHW050750190720
661023LV00006B/35/J